Kay Thomas

Not Another White Girl

To be born into whiteness is to enter a story already half-told, the ink smudged by generations of convenient silence. To be a white woman is to live as both coloniser and captive, cradled by privilege, constrained by its architect. We are the empire's afterglow, born into soft guilt and quiet advantage. Power flows through us like an ancient river that never reaches the sea. We embellish our fragility until it gleams as virtue. Has yoga become our vessel across this restless water, a borrowed language for freedom from chains we still polish?

London Yoga Press
United Kingdom
www.londonyogapress.com
@londonyogapress

Editor: Jodie McLean
Illustrator: Annabel Lobb

First edition
2025

The London Yoga Press is committed to inclusive publishing. This edition has been designed with dyslexia aware formatting for improved readability.

Copyright © 2025 London Yoga Press

All rights reserved. No part of this publication may be reproduced, stored in a retrieval system, or transmitted in any form or by any means, electronic, mechanical, photocopying, recording, or otherwise, without prior written permission of the publisher, except for brief quotations used in reviews or scholarly analysis.

ISBN: 978-1-0369-6495-5

To Patrick,
my best friend and co-conspirator in living life to the fullest.
You are the place I return to always.

ACKNOWLEDGMENTS

To **Jodie McLean**, you stepped into this manuscript as both editor and author's doula. You have that rare ability to hold both story and soul. Trimming away what no longer serves, while protecting the fragile beginnings of an idea. This book carries your fingerprints in every chapter. I admire so much the work you do with women to navigate life transitions. Your celebration of embodied pleasure is the kind of change-making this world so urgently needs. I am honoured to have your wisdom in my corner.

To **Annabel Lobb**, your creative vision brought the cover of this book to life. You have an intuitive ability to craft identity and meaning through illustration. The way you transform ideas into images, reminds us that pictures are not mere decorations but portals into our imagination. I am so grateful for your artistry.

I GRIEVE THE ART NEVER CREATED FOR FEAR OF BEING TOO CRINGE

CONTENTS

Rishikesh	1
Singapore	15
Nāda	27
Lies	43
Yoga	54
Saviour	65
Love	76
Guru	88
Seven	102
Tantra	116
Author.	128

RISHIKESH

I was raised on enchanting tales of English tea parties in mist-draped mountains, where porcelain cups clinked and tigers prowled at the garden's edge. The lace tablecloths, silver spoons, swirling steam of Darjeeling tea; every detail shimmering with a storybook glow.

   No one mentioned that our tea was soaked in the blood of plantations. Or that the linen we pressed was stitched from the suffering of the hands we were taught not to see. Long after the maps had been redrawn, something of the empire lingers in the stories we inherit. Half-remembered, half-imagined, sliding between history and fantasy, and settling, almost unnoticed, into the lullabies of memory.

I had dreamed of India for as long as I could remember. Until this invitation arrived, I circled her edges like a hesitant pilgrim. Climbing the snow-veiled mountains of Nepal, walking the white, salt-bright beaches of Sri Lanka and working inside the restless heartbeat of Bangladesh's capital. Always near but never crossing the threshold until now.

Emma and I had been friends for many years. We met as teenagers at a house party. What started as a rift over some boy had ended in me washing sick out of her hair in the bathroom sink and a lifelong friendship.

With her Jamaican and European heritage, she carries a mosaic of stories in her features, strangers often eager to place her somewhere familiar. In India, she would laugh and say that people would assume she was Indian, and sometimes she didn't bother to correct them. She is a reminder that identity is never a single story, but a tapestry of histories, migrations, and misunderstandings.

Emma's compassion is never performative but rooted in curiosity and a desire to understand the human spirit in all its complexity. She moves through life as a seeker, drawn to the edges where pain and healing meet.

Her work as a nurse and holistic practitioner mirrors her way of being in the world, both tender and unflinching. She carries a rare steadiness, able to sit with what others might turn away from.

In her company, I find myself daring to step beyond what is known. To seek not only the knowledge that pleases my appetite but also drawn to the kind that unsettles certainty. Without her, this story might never have found its first breath.

I landed at Dehradun airport in the pale light of early morning. On a small propeller plane that seemed to skid across the runway like a stone skimming water, before finally surrendering to the ground. The airport was more like a provincial bus station and there was something disarmingly welcoming about it.

Inside, the carpet was the sort you might find in your nan's living room, with a faded pattern and soft underfoot. Ceiling fans turned lazily overhead, and the few uniformed staff smiled as if genuinely pleased to see us. Outside, sunlight pressed against the glass doors. It felt like a soft landing into a slower rhythm of life.

The drive to Rishikesh wound through villages and forests, past roadside shrines painted in bright vermilion. Cows wandered unhurried across the road. By the time we reached the Akhanda Yoga Institute, the light had brightened to a gold shimmer. Emma had just completed a 200-hour yoga teacher training course, and I was staying at the school as her guest for the graduation ceremony.

The entrance to the school was a large wooden door, the kind you instinctively slow down before reaching, unsure whether to knock or bow. Shoes were left neatly in rows by the threshold and the whitewashed building curved around a courtyard blooming with bougainvillea. I felt a gentle contentment in having arrived, in the uncomplicated way that travel to new places often brings.

Not long after I arrived the celebrations begun. Emma's graduation ceremony was a luminous affair, with the *ashram* grounds filled with garlands and petals. Voices lifted in kirtan and chanting, tablas and harmoniums threading through the air. At the heart of the courtyard, students received certificates and bowed to their teachers. Each student was given a bright pink scarf, which lit up on the backdrop of their white clothes.

I stood at the edge, watching on. Assembling my objections, hunting for the fraud beneath the fragrance, scanning the scene for loose threads I could tug until the whole thing unravelled. My mind questioning how ritual and faith can be anything but illusion. A carefully choreographed pageantry, a theatre of transcendence.

Emma told stories of deities and devotion, of Ganesha removing obstacles, of Saraswati's wisdom. I nodded politely, but inside I felt a resistance, an instinctive recoil from anything that hinted at worship.

This was the same friend who had spent years defiantly rejecting her own family's Christianity. Who'd once rolled her eyes at the mention of church or prayer. Part of me wanted to laugh and whisper, *you don't actually believe all this, do you? It's just a bit of fun, right?*

And yet, what I couldn't deny was that she looked happier, radiant even. Something in her had softened or perhaps settled. She seemed lighter, less defended, as though she'd found a way to breathe more easily.

As I watched the petals float and listened to the chanting voices merge, I felt a pull. It was as though I stood at a threshold. Part sceptic and part seeker, hovering between the known architecture of doubt and what felt dangerously alive. The mind still guarded, armed and alert, but the body, traitorous and curious, had begun to lean.

Gurmukh Kaur Khalsa was one of the guests that night. I didn't know her then, only that she carried a presence that outshone her slight frame. A white woman crowned with a white turban, poised and unapologetically alive. What moved me most was her age. She was not fading into the background, as older women are so often taught to do. There was no dimming, no quiet compliance. She was vivid, as if life had ripened rather than reduced her.

She also felt familiar, a reflection, perhaps, of the same cultural permission I carried. In the West, my whiteness was unseen, unspoken, unexamined. In the East, it became a garment too bright to ignore. It trailed me like an invisible letter of recommendation; written in a language the world had long been taught to read.

The next day I woke to the sound of distant chanting, a rhythm that seemed to rise with the mist from the Ganga. Drawn by friendship and wonder, I had landed in Rishikesh, the world capital of yoga. A mirror for every Western projection of holiness.

To walk through its streets is to move through a living collage. The scent of incense curling through diesel fumes. Cows linger in the road, eyes half-closed, aware that even the chaos would bow to their holiness. Orange-robed sadhus blessing tourists for a few rupees. Monkeys patrol the rooftops and swing from power lines, their hands quick and deliberate as they steal fruit from the hands of the unwary.

Ashrams rise one after another along the banks of the Ganga, painted in pastel pinks and yellows, each promising a different kind of salvation. The chants of *Om Namah Shivaya* float from loudspeakers, mingling with the honks of motorbikes and the calls of chai sellers.

Down by the water, the chaos softens. The Ganga moves with her own slow authority, a vein of green and silver light. The *Vedas* speak of the river Ganga not as water, but as divinity in motion. A goddess descending from the heavens to cleanse the world. Devotees step into her current, clutching the iron chains fixed to the stone steps to keep from being swept away. Some murmur prayers, others stand silently.

At the water's edge, devotion and daily life weave together with ease. The same steps where pilgrims pray also become filled with families and companions who linger long after the sun has set.

Rishikesh is not only a place of pilgrimage; it is a holiday destination. Visitors stroll the ghats with paper cups, buying gifts and enjoying each other's company. I watch a man balance his phone on a railing, framing his family against the beauty of a city that hums with prayer and laughter in equal measure. Nearby, friends wade into the shallows, splashing each other with mock shrieks, their joy unselfconscious.

There is a lightness here, the same kind that lingers in seaside towns on English shores. I caught a glimpse of home, not as geography, but as a memory. Each summer we would join the crowds of Londoners crammed onto trains bound for Brighton beach, seeking the promise of sea air and salty chips. The day would feel like an exhale of breath and in these moments of shared joy, there was a kind of holiness. Not the kind taught in temples, but the divinity of people briefly freed from the weight of their lives.

The next day we bought tickets to the International Yoga Festival, held at the Parmarth Niketan Ashram. A sanctuary that would later come to anchor my time in Rishikesh. That morning, the air buzzed with anticipation. Pilgrims and influencers moved side by side through the ashram gates, yoga mats slung over shoulders, a sea of linen, mala beads, and essential oils. Loudspeakers announced the day's sessions.

The festival was a kind of Disneyland for yogis. Teachers from across the globe, returning to the motherland with fresh ideas and modern interpretations. We drifted from shamanic healing to gut-health talks, from chakra cleansing to sound baths. I loved it, swept up in the colour and wonder of it all.

The Parmarth Niketan Ashram has an ability to hold many versions of devotion with genuine openness. The International Yoga Festival amplified this diversity. A kaleidoscope of traditions, each arriving with its own history, its own beliefs, its own blind spots.

Then it arrived, like a sharp slap to the face. On

the stage stood an anti-abortion sign. My stomach turned. The air thickened. I felt the hairs on my arms rise, as if my body recognised something before my mind did. *How had I been so trusting, so careless with my belonging?* I wanted to run, to wash the association from my skin.

Emma agreed to move on to another workshop, but her composure unsettled me. I wanted her to feel what I felt, the sting of betrayal. The sudden feeling that beneath the language of love and light, control had disguised itself as devotion.

My anger took on the shape of something moral; it felt earned, even necessary, as if I had been appointed judge and jury. In my fury, I was not merely upset, I was right. Emma's steadiness, her refusal to burn alongside me, felt like a failure of allegiance.

Then in Emma's reflection, I caught a glimpse of myself. The swiftness with which I divide the world into right and wrong. How easily I cast myself as the hero in a story of my own making. In her calm I felt the unspoken authority of someone who knew me well enough not to flatter my fury.

Our friendship, long enough to have weathered many versions of ourselves and as she stood there with no agenda, I could clearly see my own. Able to witness my ego. And in that moment, feel gratitude for the warning it had delivered, and then let it pass. Rather than clutching it like a trophy of accomplishment. I felt my breath deepen and presence return.

We wandered for a while, letting the tide of the crowd carry us, until we slipped into a large white marquee, red carpet underfoot and a stage at the front. The petite woman in the white turban I had noticed at the graduation ceremony the day before appeared on stage.

Her class that day was unlike any yoga class I had attended before. There were no mirrors, no tidy rows of postures to master. Gurmukh began by asking us to sit cross-legged, eyes closed, palms pressed together at the heart centre. She spoke softly at first, her voice carrying a Californian thread and a touch of something that didn't come from geography.

"You are not your thoughts; you are the one who watches them pass," she said. We chanted *Sat Nam*, over and over, until the syllables became sound rather than meaning. The movements were primal, arms raised, twisting, pulsing, breath drawn

sharp through the nose and released like fire. It wasn't about elegance; it was about endurance and eventually surrendering.

The tent smelled of rosewater and sweat. My shoulders burned, my lungs protested, and still she urged us on. *"Keep going! Ten more breaths! Burn through the doubt!"* The drumming quickened. A storm of bodies. Breath, laughter and tears: indistinguishable. And then stillness.

A silence so sudden it felt like being inhaled into the universe itself. I could feel my breath, deliberate and expanding into the space where sound had been. My heart pounding against the floor with each inhale, the last trace of the chant still humming behind my ribs.

The experience bypassed thought entirely. It arrived through the skin, into the lungs, reaching into the space behind the sternum. For a few suspended moments I wasn't analysing or striving, just breathing. When the sound finally returned, something in me had rearranged itself, as though a door had been left ajar. A new energy stirred within me; one I hoped would outlast the walls of the tent.

Before leaving Rishikesh, I packed my bags with

books gathered from the shops that lined its winding streets. One of these books was *The Eight Human Talents* by Gurmukh.

My devotion to this book became almost biblical. The cover soon creased and softened from use, the pages peppered with notes and tea stains. I read it everywhere, in cafés, on the metro, by the glow of my phone in my marital bed. I underlined lines in the book not to remember them but to inhabit them, to invite their meaning to move beyond intellect and take root in my lived experience.

I was searching for a version of yoga that I could belong to. I found myself clutching at *Kuṇḍalinī Yoga* like a lifeline, its chants, its white cotton, its rituals. There was something magnetic about it.

Listening to the mantra, I felt a peace settle over me. From this sacred sound, I found a release from the anxieties that had begun to coil behind the façade I was carrying. Instead of reaching for the small white tablets before every flight, I could now slip on my headphones and feel the fear loosen its grip. As if the sound itself had become a kind of medicine.

These teachings, with all their beauty and

rhythm, flowed from the heart of the Sikh faith. A religion rooted in the land of 15th-century Punjab. Centuries later, fragments of this spiritual heritage were now being carried to me through the medium of white Western women. Their chants were pronounced with practiced ease and their turbans worn with perfect precision.

I began to wonder if this path, reshaped through distant hands and histories, still held the truth it claimed. At first, I saw this caution as discernment. My gracefulness in being careful with what was sacred. Dressed in my virtue, wearing this instinct to question, to hold myself slightly apart and bow at the altar of my own sense of self.

Then another truth rippled into view. One that did not question their authenticity, but the flags I was parading around my own. I could see the lineage of ideas I'd inherited whispering at the edges.

Ancient cartographers of the mind, sketching their maps of the world, assigning borders, deciding what appears authentic and who is permitted to belong. And perhaps this is why my path had led me here, an invitation to face the empire living inside of me. To recognise its architecture, and to let its walls begin to fall.

The gift I carried home from Rishikesh was not enlightenment, nor certainty, but a new willingness to sit with my own contradictions. I was no longer merely passing through the world hunting for proof and demanding answers. I was beginning, gently, to listen and feel for what was beneath the identity I claimed.

SINGAPORE

When I accepted the invitation to Rishikesh, my life was rooted in the small shimmering island of Singapore. Newly married, we had moved there as a sort of marital compromise, my yearning to travel meeting my husband's desire to build a life for the future. I had not yet understood how deeply the title of expat wife would unsettle my sense of self.

Once fiercely independent, I now lived under a dependent visa, with little to fill my days beyond chocolate-making classes with other wives, and the unspoken pressure to have dinner ready before he came home from work.

We travelled often, skipping between islands and white-sand beaches on weekends. From the outside, it was idyllic. But I would come to learn that once comfort and safety are met, happiness refuses to be curated, not even by the most perfect sunsets or the bluest sea.

Patrick and I met at university. He was at Oxford, and I was at the polytechnic down the road. Never one to shy away from an opinion, I joined the Oxford Debating Society. Where after one Thursday night debate our paths crossed on a sticky dance floor at a bar called The Bridge.

He was, and still is, one of the kindest and most brilliant people I know, a mathematician with a mind of pure logic and a heart that means no harm. And this, I believe, is why it took me such a long time to admit that I was miserable. Patrick's mind moves in elegant equations, but sometimes logic leaves little room for human messiness and longing. We began to drift. I felt trapped, weighed down by guilt, because it had been my idea to move abroad and he had worked tirelessly to make it possible.

I thought perhaps getting a job might help, might make me feel like myself again. I found work at a charity providing free healthcare to migrant workers. Men who had travelled from Bangladesh and India, seeking opportunity but often finding debt and confinement. They lived in dormitories on the edge of the island, vast concrete blocks that housed thousands. Their lives were hemmed in by curfews and contracts.

Each morning, I arrived before dawn to open the shutters of our small clinic, and already the queue would stretch around the block. A line of men waited patiently in the heat, clutching slips of paper, empty medicine packets, and pleas for help. Inside, the day moved fast, the kind of pace that leaves no room for thought.

As I pulled down the shutters each night, my eyes met the faces of those we had to turn away. Come back tomorrow I would say in a tone of promise, but the weight of their disappointment settled like rain-filled clouds beckoning a storm inside.

Beneath the glass towers and manicured streets lay a truth the skyline refused to speak of. A city built on the backs of those whose names would never be known. The job had given me purpose again, a glimpse of myself beyond the role of wife, but it had come at a cost. Slowly stripping away the glossy veneer of a country I was trying to call home.

In the year we arrived in Singapore, new rules were tightening around those of us on dependent visas. They felt like invisible walls, stricter quotas, higher salary thresholds, layers of paperwork that seemed designed to remind you that you did not belong outside the shopping malls. I sent out hundreds of applications, with deafening silence.

When this job finally surfaced, I clung to it with the desperation of someone gasping for air. So much so that when the CEO insisted on speaking to my husband for his permission before I could accept the job, I pushed down the anger curling in my gut.

The request felt like it had slipped through a crack in time, dragged in from another century. I did try to push back, asking whether he would ask the same if I were a man. He smiled through clenched teeth, but we both knew the answer.

Salvation found me each week in the form of a yoga class. Patrick had started coming with me, and in those hours, I felt close to him again. As we laughed together, red-faced, at our inability to touch our toes.

Our teacher, Pam, was this beautifully sweet

Singaporean woman. She had radiant joyfulness that lulled you in with ease, but she should have been enlisted by the Singaporean army because she took no prisoners in her classes. We bent, twisted, and held to her command, with our legs trembling as she smiled serenely and said, *"remember to breathe".*

The studio felt like something out of Los Angeles, all glass, greenery, and curated calm. Rows of identical mats, candles flickering in copper bowls, the faint scent of lemongrass in the air. I arrived each week in my Lululemon uniform. The brand that had turned mindfulness into an aesthetic. I told myself I was there for peace, but part of me knew I was also there to look like I had found it.

We got to know Pam well and began spending evenings together. Singaporeans often hesitate to befriend expats because the transience makes relationships fragile, but Pam was different. Though born and bred in Singapore, she existed on the edge of what was expected, in her thirties and unmarried. In a society that rewarded early coupling, she was an outlier.

In Singapore, marriage is not merely a union; it is a kind of citizenship. The city's housing laws reveal this devotion clearly; love recognised by the state comes with a key and a view. Pam once told us, half-laughing, half-resigned, that as a single woman she would have to wait until thirty-five to buy a government flat, while married couples were handed that right in their twenties.

Singaporeans are kind and gentle people, with a quiet politeness stitched into everyday gestures. Offering a seat, shifting aside in a corridor or a soft word exchanged on the metro. But beneath that calm runs an undercurrent of caution and fear.

Every year, the sirens come alive across the island. A single pulsing note, like an invocation of war. They are used not just for real emergencies but also for public awareness drills. It is a rehearsal, a reminder to never stop being vigilant. Posters adorn the streets with the slogan, *"NOT IF, BUT WHEN."*

Singapore is a fortress, bracing against the anticipated threat from the other. Sandwiched between the unpredictable politics of Malaysia and the vastness of Indonesia. Emerging from the turbulence of decolonisation, Lee Kuan Yew built a nation with the vigilance of a man who knew how quickly small islands could be swallowed whole when the tides of global power change.

Safety is worn with pride, stitched into the nation's fabric. People leave their mobile phones to reserve tables in hawker centres, a silent declaration of trust in their society. As someone who had grown up gripping her phone tight on the streets of South London, it felt like stepping into a different version of reality.

On the surface it was a kind of utopia, with spotless pavements, efficient systems, and a beautiful skyline. But beauty, when too perfectly arranged, can begin to feel like a rehearsal rather than real life. I thought of yin and yang, the dance of opposites keeping the world in motion. Safety had been achieved, but at the cost of something raw and human. That friction, that disordered imperfection, had been exiled.

At the far edge of the island, where the highways thin into quiet roads, I found a piece of something that refused to be tamed. Bollywood Veggies was a reminder that life could still grow without supervision. My weekends had been a blur of glossy towers, manicured parks, air-conditioned cafés where even the conversation felt climate controlled. But here, Singapore gave way to something tropical and free.

It wasn't so much a farm, more a rebellion that happened to grow bananas. Its founder, Ivy Singh-Lim, called herself *"The Gentle Warrior"*. She'd once led Singapore's netball team and later turned her energy to the land, defying every polite expectation placed on women of her generation.

She spoke openly about politics, patriarchy, and the sanitisation of society. About how Singapore had become efficient but fearful. Her farm became her protest. Against hierarchy, against the silent, compliant erasure of the unruly and imperfect. Feminism in her world wasn't theory; it was compost and courage.

To call her eccentric is to miss the point. She is fierce, foul-mouthed and gloriously unfiltered. What struck me first at Bollywood Veggies wasn't the banana trees, but the signs. They hang from fences, trees, and bamboo posts, handwritten in bold strokes of yellow on green boards, each one a declaration of independence. *"No idiots allowed,"* one warns cheerfully. Another proclaims, *"You cannot serve both God and Money."* Some were political, *"We Do Not Fear Terrorists! We have Politicians."* They are part manifesto, part mischief,

Ivy's voice in technicolour echoing across the farm.

In Singapore, protest is not only frowned upon but forbidden, it is technically illegal without a permit. Permission is rarely granted to maintain the narrative of order. To speak against authority is to step out of rhythm with the city's carefully composed harmony.

Yet Ivy Singh-Lim dares to paint her dissent in plain view. Her words nailed to the walls of her farm like open secrets. Perhaps she survives because she cloaks rebellion in humour, because her fire is tempered by the charisma of age and eccentricity. Each of her signs is a small uprising, brushstrokes of truth in a landscape where silence has long been the safest currency.

I found myself suspended between two worlds, one foot in the glitter of expat life, the other in the shadowed back rooms that made it possible. I moved through penthouse apartments and rooftop pools, but then at dinner parties, the façade would crack at the edges. A housemaid lingering near the kitchen door, eyes lowered, her exhaustion unmistakable if you took the time to look.

Desperate to find some sense of belonging in this paradox of existence, I joined the Reiki Centre.

The classes were an unusual blend of locals and expats, people who didn't seem to fit neatly anywhere. The mix felt honest, less about where you were from and more about what you were trying to heal.

I trained under Karen Taylor, a British-born teacher whose parents had lived across continents; her accent softened by travel. She carried a gentleness that never tipped into fragility. Before discovering Reiki, she had worked as a hypnotherapist, and her teaching carried that same steady cadence of calm, certainty, and gentle persuasion.

Karen spoke about experiments suggesting that Reiki could alter the molecular structure of water. She mentioned the work of a Japanese researcher, Dr Masaru Emoto, who claimed that water exposed to loving words and music formed delicate, symmetrical crystals when frozen. Whilst water spoken to with anger was said to produce chaotic, fractured shapes. The idea fascinated me, the possibility that thought itself could leave an imprint on matter, that intention might ripple outward in ways unseen. It sounded improbable, but it also felt poetic.

I wanted to believe there was a connection between the unseen and the tangible, between what we feel and what we become. Still anchored in my logical brain, I found comfort in the science of it, or at least the illusion of science. It allowed me to flirt with faith without betraying reason, to step a little closer to the mystery while keeping one foot on solid ground.

Reiki offered me connection, and Bollywood Veggies a glimpse of freedom, but my life in Singapore soon crept back to routine. The days blurred into the rhythm of work, weekends and dinner plans, the same invisible cage I had tried to escape from in London. I had travelled halfway across the world searching for transformation but found instead a subtler truth, geography cannot rewrite the self.

The more I questioned my own compliance, the more the women on the island revealed themselves in small acts of rebellion. Pam, with her quiet strength, bent tradition without ever announcing it. Karen, with her gentleness, guided strangers toward healing. And Ivy, fierce and unapologetic, refused every script ever handed to her. They had each, in their own way, carved out lives that made room for their truth rather than tightening themselves to fit expectations.

Illuminating, how easily I had stepped into the role of expat wife, as if it were the only shape available, folding myself into its narrow corners. The women around me were living proof that compliance was not the only currency a woman could trade in. They showed me that a woman's life does not have to be ordained, it can be authored.

Patrick still believed that happiness could be engineered, that with enough logic and willpower life's joy would rise obediently from the plans we made.

Maybe I just needed to try harder, silence the storms inside me, bury my doubts deeper. Be more positive. But my own contentment seemed to live in the cracks between plans. I longed for an adventure into the unknown. Craving the thrill of possibility, the kind that reminds you that you are alive.

Like every seeker with a backpack and no plan. I wanted to find myself.

NĀDA

One evening, in my apartment in Singapore, restless and searching, I typed *"Yoga teacher training in Rishikesh"* into Google.

It had been 9 months since I'd visited Emma. Among the many offerings that appeared on the screen, one caught my eye, the Nāda Yoga School. I didn't know it then, but that click was the start of an adventure not across continents, but through the wild terrain of my own sense of self.

Patrick and I had not been apart for more than a few days since we had met almost a decade earlier. Yet somehow, we had begun to live on opposite shores of the same sea. There is a loneliness that has nothing to do with being alone;

it arrives quietly, settling between two people who still share the same bed.

The colours of life had tinged a shade of grey. We didn't argue. We simply stopped talking, except for the practical exchanges that kept life running. Those small logistics that can pass for intimacy.

Staring into the harsh glow of the laptop screen, I realised that I was frightened to be alone. Not the simple, passing kind of fear, but the kind that seeps into mornings and makes a new day feel like a task rather than a beginning.

My sense of self had shrunk into something I barely recognised. A tight circle of routines was slowly suffocating me. Loneliness had stopped being an absence and was beginning to feel like a presence, one that pressed against my ribs and made it hard to breathe.

Beneath the fear, a small, stubborn flame flickered for my attention. A whisper of possibility, tugged at me. The voice grew louder and insisting, *something has to change!* I could not keep living inside the hollow of my own fear. Before I could talk myself out of it, before caution reclaimed its seat beside me, I booked a one-month teacher training course at the Nāda Yoga School.

The course began on New Year's Eve, a clean line drawn between what had been and what might be. Electric excitement pulsed through me, reminding me of packing my bags for the first year at university. That rare, delicious sense that life was about to begin again.

Part of me longed for transformation, and yet another part was uneasy at what it might cost. Beneath the excitement, I was nervous, not of the place itself, but of what might awaken in the silence of these practices. The truths that wait patiently beneath the noise of our lives.

As my taxi wrestled the traffic bound for Rishikesh, a tremor of excited anticipation threaded itself through my body. The town unfolding around me in its familiar mix of colourful enchantment.

One of the boys from the Nāda Yoga School, Mohan, met me from the taxi. A gentle smile cut through the chaos and I climbed onto the back of his motorbike. My heavy hiking backpack pressed awkwardly between us, we wove through the narrow streets and out toward the river. As we approached, I could see the shimmer of the Ganga, and high above the mountains holding their steady, watchful gaze.

Weaving across the Ram Jhula bridge, swerving between people and cows. The smells, the colours, the noise seemed to envelop me, rising around me like a living current. I felt wide awake inside the moment that had finally found me.

The bike came to a stop on the cobbled street just after the bridge. Set into the curve of a stone wall a metal gate led into a small courtyard wrapping itself protectively around a sacred fig tree. The building looked more like a house than a school. A single storey with white stone walls and wicker chairs on the porch. The wooden doors and shutters were thick with layers of paint. I pushed the door open and stepped inside. Some of the students on my course had already arrived and were sitting around a table.

And then, without warning, a strange sensation swept over me, not metaphorical, but startlingly physical. My eyes moved across the room, but it was my body that recognised it first. A wave of familiarity rose through me, so complete it made my skin prickle. Every detail of the inbuilt bookshelves carved into the walls was known, the shape of the window, position of the doors all known. My mind scrambled to make sense of it, anxious to rationalise before I lost my footing.

Perhaps I was overtired from the journey. Was this some kind of mild hallucination? I'd never experienced déjà vu, and anyone who spoke of past lives, I privately filed alongside those who believed in ghosts. To be totally honest, I thought people only said such things when a place felt vaguely familiar, romanticising coincidence into destiny.

The recognition was so sudden it caught in my throat. I felt tears rising but swallowed them back. Not from embarrassment, but from fear that someone might notice and ask me to name what I couldn't explain. I had no framework for what I was feeling. Just as I was hoping the ground might swallow me up, Rohit introduced himself and asked if he could show me to my room.

Every great place has its anchor, the one who steadies the vessel when no one else is watching. At the school, this is Rohit. He manages the bookings, absorbs the relentless questions, and meets every request with an unwavering calm.

I followed him out through the lanes to the living quarters in Swargashram, tucked just along from the school. At the entrance of the building stood a giant statue of the Hindu god Shiva (Śiva).

Seated crossed-legged and supported by a plinth dusted with marigolds and ash, his skin was the colour of deep water, blushing into shades of violet where the sun touched him. A crescent moon curved against his long dark hair and serpents coiled at his throat. His face serene, but his body carved in unapologetic power. Every muscle caught in tension, while a narrow strip of cloth slung across his groin.

Long before Hinduism learned his name, he moved through the Vedic world as Rudra, fierce and untamed. Then whispered into being in the hymns (*sūktas*) of the *Rig Veda*, one of the oldest sacred texts.

Over centuries, this wild god learned stillness and was reimagined as Shiva (Śiva), becoming the meditative, erotic, and cosmic figure before me. In Indian philosophy, sexual energy is sacred life-force, not something to hide.

Standing there, I thought of an article I had read on the flight in an English newspaper. It described how the digital age had transformed the way readers purchased erotic fiction: no cashier, no queue, no risk of being seen. With a click of a button, curiosity could be satisfied in private. Sales had surged, and with them a shift in fantasy itself. The most popular stories were no longer grounded in realism, but flooded with the supernatural, werewolves, vampires, fairies, and other fantasies of desire.

The boom had grown so dominant, the article claimed, that whispers circulated of Amazon revising its book categories altogether. Creating new filters and sub-genres simply to stop fantasy creatures from overrunning the bestseller lists. I smiled to myself wondering if all these people knew the streets of Rishikesh were filled with so much gold.

Rohit opened the door, inside the lilac room were two single beds and to my surprise, on one of them sat Tanya. I'm the sort of person who assembles things without reading the instructions, who clicks 'consent' without ever glancing at the terms and conditions. What was not a surprise, was that when I booked the course, I had failed to read the note that rooms were shared unless otherwise requested.

I would have assumed my adult self would long

for privacy, but what I felt in that moment was relief. Without quite knowing it, the thought of spending a month in a room alone had filled me with dread. I grew up as an only child between two homes, loved deeply and separately by each of my parents, their affection wrapping me so closely that solitude still felt like a kind of freefall.

Tanya was from Germany. She had a strong energy, clear, steady and assured. I liked her directness; it made me feel safe. Her energy didn't swirl or perform. And something in me, long accustomed to arriving in costume, unfastened my mask.

She was comfortable with silence in a way that I was not. And there, in our simple room, when my small talk faded, and she didn't try to fill the quiet, I found myself beginning to reflect.

Echoing in the far corners of my mind, like the dull pulse of a migraine, was the question: *How has it taken you so long to come home?* It was quickly met by another voice, sharp and mocking: *Get a grip girlie, you're one step away from buying crystals and asking people's star signs before their names.*

My mind raced to intellectualise what had

happened at the school earlier. Could it have been some form of somatic memory rising from a forgotten corner of my body. Or, maybe, a simple Gestalt familiarity, my mind weaving patterns together faster than thought and recognising the architecture of a place I'd never actually seen.

As I sat in the silence another truth settled over me. I hadn't come here to untangle theories or win arguments with myself. I'd arrived because somewhere inside me, there was a hunger to feel alive. I needed the part of my brain that had seen me through an economics degree, the part that took comfort in the tangible and the measurable, to take a holiday. It was time to sit in the discomfort, to sweat it out and see what might be waiting beneath the logic.

That night at dinner, someone in our group suggested we go down to a café near Laxman Jhula bridge to welcome the new year. Buddha Café perched high above the river, its bamboo walls and dangling lights giving it the feel of a treehouse suspended in the sky. Rishikesh is considered a holy pilgrimage town, and the local government enforces strict bans on alcohol and non-vegetarian food within its municipal limits.

This would be the first New Year's Eve I had spent sober since I was a teenager, a thought that landed with a striking chill. We drank herbal tea and sat cross-legged on low cushions, getting to know one another as the band tuned up at the front. When they called for volunteers for the open mic, we all turned to Josh, a singer among us, nudging him forward with laughter and cheers.

The room fell silent, Josh's voice was pure and unguarded, the kind of sound that doesn't just reach you but moves through you. As I caught the eyes of my group, our faces softened into smiles. I had come to Rishikesh to learn yoga through the medium of sound and vibration, and that night felt like my first lesson.

The music had formed a bridge between souls; we were no longer strangers. As I looked around the room, I saw how different we were on paper, a tapestry of ages, languages, and histories. Yet the same invisible thread had drawn us all here, to the banks of the Ganga. It was the beginning of a month that would bind us together, a beautiful, improbable family, born at the Nāda Yoga School.

The next morning, our teacher and founder of the school led the first class. Bhuwanji sat at the front of the class, not above us, but perched on the edge of the stage. He wore a plain, Western-style zip-up hoodie; no mala beads, no signs of holiness. There was no aura of ceremony around him, only a kind, approachable presence.

He spoke of *nāda brahma*, the ancient belief that creation began not with light, but with sound. Before stars were born or forms took shape, there was vibration. In the Vedas, it is written that the universe itself was sung into being, that every atom carries the faint echo of that primordial note. Bhuwanji's voice softened as he explained that when we chant, when we listen, when we breathe in rhythm, we are tracing our way back to the pulse of existence itself.

Like many who have attended a yoga class before, I was familiar with the ritual of chanting *Om (Aum ॐ)* at the beginning or end of a session. I had only ever repeated the sound without understanding its depth. It was an echo of something ancient, stripped of its context, a habit rather than a prayer.

Bhuwanji taught us that in yoga philosophy, it is not a symbol but a frequency, the pulse that holds the universe together. To chant it is to align the finite rhythm of the body with the infinite rhythm of creation.

I thought of the physics I half remembered from school, how everything moves in waves, how sound travels through air, how energy is never lost, only passed along. Scientists, too, speak of energy that never dies, only changes form, not so different from the ancient sages who said that all matter is condensed sound. Perhaps, the language of faith and the language of science had never really been at odds. They were simply telling the same story in different dialects.

When the class began to chant, the sound was rough at first, a roomful of strangers fumbling for unity. But as the tones deepened, something shifted. The vibration filled the walls, travelled through the floorboards, and found its way into my chest. For a moment I couldn't tell where my voice ended, and the others began.

When the final voice faded, it didn't end, rather, it dissolved into a hush that seemed alive. No one spoke. I felt the sound lingering beneath my skin. The silence that followed was not empty but full, humming with invisible order. At that moment, I understood why it was called the sound of the universe. It wasn't a concept or a metaphor; it was presence, vast, unhurried, and strangely familiar.

I thought of how I'd come here searching for answers. And yet, sitting in that room, I no longer needed words at all. My mind, trained to analyse, finally loosened its grip. The rational part of me was no longer trying to label it. The part of me that felt, the part I had been ignoring for so long, simply wanted to stay there, suspended in that shared stillness.

As part of our *Nāda Yoga* course, each of us was given the choice of an instrument to study. I chose the harmonium; its soulful tone reminded me of the accordion in old folk songs, full of longing and mystery. I had arrived with no musical training, so in a childlike way I began to draw out the keys in my notebook. Sketching rough diagrams of scales and sequences so I could picture what my hands were meant to do. It was clumsy but strangely liberating, a reminder that learning isn't just about mastering a method, but about finding a way.

Bhuwanji was endlessly patient. He seemed to hold a confidence that learning happens in its own time, like a seed that sprouts only when the soil is ready. He gave me the freedom to find my own route, to learn through feeling rather than form. Offering his expertise only when I reached for it. There was no pressure, no hierarchy, only a gentle confidence that I would get there, eventually.

The school itself seemed to deliver knowledge intuitively. Every student came with a different story, and the teaching adapted. There was no rigid curriculum, no standardised outcome to reach. In the West, we are so used to instruction being bound by frameworks, measurable progress, and learning outcomes that anything less constrained, at first, feels like chaos.

Here, the absence of structure was its own kind of teaching. What could look like disorder to the Western gaze, was in fact responsiveness. The teacher attuning to the student in front of them, allowing the learning to unfold in its own rhythm. To be seen by a teacher in this way bypasses performance and awakens participation.

In the evenings, we gathered for kirtan, where music turned into devotion. The room would fill with the rhythmic beat of the tabla, the swell of harmoniums, and the shimmer of bells. Singing tentatively at first, my British reserve wrapped tight around my throat. But slowly something began to shift. I learned to sing with surrender, to let the sound move through me rather than control it.

I had believed that devotion belonged to religion, to doctrine, to the approved architecture of belief. But in that candlelit room, devotion had nothing to do with obedience. It was not a conscious belief in a god, but a sensation of the divine awakening inside the body. It lived in the shared breath, the shared beat, the shared willingness to return again and again to the mantra.

It wasn't sung so much as it poured itself into the air. Simple syllables, repeated like a fisherman casting the same net into deeper and deeper water. A tide pulling us inward. I watched how it made faces changed, frown lines softened and jaws unclenched.

There comes a point in kirtan when the rhythm lifts, and the room tips into something that feels like flight. The tabla quickens; the harmoniums gather speed; voices stretch beyond the shape of syllables. A collective ecstasy that cannot be manufactured or easily explained. It arrives when the ego begins to dissolve at the edges, shedding the armour of the 'self,' the 'individual,' the 'I'. And you feel yourself melting into the shared consciousness.

When the music exhaled its final breath, the silence settled around us like the warm embrace of sunshine on a cold day. The architecture of my old self loosened its grip and loneliness slipped away without protest. Leaving behind the luminous echo of belonging.

I began to sense how much of my life had been lived from the neck up. Governed by explanation; defended by reason. *Nāda Yoga* offered a different orientation. It asked me to listen before I spoke, to feel before I named, to trust that not everything meaningful arrives dressed as certainty. Sound was teaching me what words could not.

I was learning to listen, to the vibration, to the silence, to the spaces between. I felt a subtle rewiring of attention. A recalibration of the self. Less guarded, more porous to the world.

The fear that had once pressed against my ribs had loosened its grip. A new willingness to stay present with what is, without trying to fix or flee. Nāda Yoga didn't change my life by adding something new, it did so by revealing what had always been there, waiting patiently for me.

LIES

One evening down by the river, as the chanting from *arti (ārati)* at the nearby ashram faded and the river returned to its low, continuous murmur. I found myself tracing the veins of my own history. I pictured the map of a girl born from a nation that once sought to rule and control this land, now on her knees, pleading for the secrets it holds.

An email from Cambridge University's Centre of South Asian Studies sat unopened in my inbox. Waiting inside were my great-grandfather's memoirs, a voice from a world I carried in my DNA but never fully claimed. I had always believed that the world I grew up in bore no resemblance to my colonial ancestry. Now here in India, I began to wonder if the distance between them was thinner than I wanted to admit. Maybe the roots I thought were long severed had been quietly threading themselves through my life all along.

Until the age of eight, I had grown up in the White House on the Clapham Park Estate in South London. The name suggests elegance, something stately, dignified. In truth, it was a tired council block where cement flaked from the walls without warning and the windows shivered at the hint of wind. The glass was thin as paper, and mould gathered freely in the corners, claiming the place as its own. The lift broke down often, and the corridors were perfumed with the fragrance of urine.

Life there had its own rhythm. The neighbours upstairs would play loud music at night, the bass vibrating through the ceiling until the early hours. When we complained, they spat on our door. Once, a woman threw the entire contents of her flat out of the window, screaming about another woman as clothes and crockery rained down like a storm.

Not all of our neighbours were feral. Across the landing lived Akee, a tall, soft-spoken black man.

He always smiled and asked if we were alright. I remember thinking that if anything bad ever happened, I could knock on his door.

For all its decay, the estate had pockets of beauty. Green spaces woven between the buildings, chestnut trees heavy with conkers, their roots cracking through the concrete. I didn't know it then, but even there, in a place built on neglect, I was learning how beauty survives, how life insists on growing through the cracks.

My primary school sat at the edge of the estate. A low, sprawling post-war prefab with long bands of glass that let the light spill into every corridor. Brushed with the optimism of post-war modernism, where space was prioritised over grandeur. Wide open playgrounds and grass lawns breaking up the tarmac.

Inside those walls the faces were a mosaic of the world, a map contained within a single building. Diversity existed without instruction. It was not an ideal, but the ordinary fabric of the place, shaping the rhythm of everyday. I spoke with an accent that didn't belong to my postcode. It wasn't the voice of the estate, perhaps a faint echo of my colonial ancestry. A voice that, throughout my life, would bring both privilege and judgement. But at that age, no one thought much of it. Children, still innocent of the entrenched British class system, simply decided I had an accent.

Our teachers worked tirelessly to expand our imaginations, to show us that the borders of the estate were not the borders of our minds. They slipped us glimpses of other worlds in books and poems. In doing so, they planted the first seeds of questioning, that would grow long after the lessons ended, reaching far beyond those classroom walls.

Sitting cross-legged on the cold, polished wooden floor of the school hall, was the first time I heard the words from John Agard's poem *Half-Caste*. The gymnasium apparatus of climbing frames, ropes and wooden benches, stacked neatly at the side like resting giants. Sunlight flooded through high windows, catching dust motes that drifted lazily in the air.

Our headteacher stood at the front, as she began to read, her voice echoed around the hall, gathering strength as the poem took hold. An entire hall of small, restless bodies fell quiet, captivated by the words that drifted through the air. I can now see the poem landed like a moral awakening. Until then, I'd used the word as easily as my classmates did and said it without a thought for its meaning.

It was the first time I caught a glimpse that racism didn't just live in history books, and that even a word, spoken lightly, could carry centuries inside it. It was the beginning of a kind of seeing, the slow unpeeling of the world I'd inherited. The English I spoke so fluently carried the weight of history inside its words, and the long shadow of colonialism inside its stories.

I have continued to learn how the words I grew up with carry invisible hierarchies. They live quietly in metaphors of light and dark, good and bad. Never naming the bias beneath. Rarely does this feel more charged than in the phrase *white lie*. A term used to describe a harmless untruth, framed as kindness over honesty. Although the colour's origins weren't explicitly tied to race, its continued use is questionable.

What seems like an innocent idiom reveals something deeper. How the moral imagination of the West is tinted by colour. How purity became entwined with whiteness itself. These aren't just habits of speech. They are echoes of an older story, one where light was worshipped and darkness feared. Where even honesty and guilt were divided by shade.

Like much of our history, the narrative is shaped by those who hold the pen. Nations, too, have hidden behind their own mythologies of benevolence. Britain, once the richest empire on earth, limped out of the Second World War, borrowing heavily from the United States just to survive. It could not bear to name its decline. Instead, it choreographed its withdrawal from India as generosity, handing out freedom with the theatre of a benefactor, while counting its debts beneath the table.

That performance of benevolence still echoes in the Western psyche. We inherited the story of the empire's glory, not its insolvency. Even now, the figure of the white traveller arrives trailing the scent of that history. The assumption of wealth, of means, of belonging to a lineage that conquered and gave. In truth many of us are quietly drowning in debt, carrying the invisible burden of loans and the restless pressure to maintain a life we cannot truly afford.

Lying on my firm mattress in the ashram that night, with the ceiling fan whirling above with comforting monotony. I opened my great-grandfather's memoirs. He had been a general manager for the Burma Oil Company, living in Rangoon, until the Japanese invasion during the Second World War, when they fled to India.

Reading his words felt like placing my face against a windowpane that looks back into another world.

"As the Japs advanced up the country, we had to destroy and escape, which we did. The great majority of the British staff were staunch, and did what was required of them without panic or weakness, but there were exceptions. I do not remember any exceptions among the Anglo-Burman or Anglo-Indian personnel. Readers of Kipling who do not know the East at first hand may well have formed an impression that the half-caste in India was a poor type, with weakness of both races. My own experience was very different, they were upstanding, honest and vigorous types and none of them let us down in this trying time. They were of course used to a lower standard of living than we were, and in that sense were better prepared for the hardship of evacuation."

A glimpse into the brutal urgency of evacuation in wartime Burma, but also into the moral architecture of the empire he served, its loyalties, hierarchies, and assumptions. I was proud to read his praise of the Anglo-Burman and Anglo-Indian personnel, not least because it pushed against the prejudices of his time.

There is a genuine respect in his tone, admiration for their resilience, their honesty, their conduct under pressure. It contradicts the lazy caricatures that British society absorbed and stands as a correction from someone who lived alongside them rather than writing from afar.

However, woven through his generosity, the language exposes its era. *"Used to a lower standard of living,"* he writes, framing endurance not as a product of culture, community, or character, but as a side effect of deprivation. It is the logic of empire, to admire while still placing oneself above. A reminder of how discrimination often hides behind the comforting illusion of fairness. Cloaked in language that reassures the speaker more than it liberates the subject.

These memoirs are both a record and a mirror. They force me to look at the scaffolding of ideas that shaped my lineage, the hierarchies passed down in tone and phrasing as much as in blood. They remind me that history is written through the eyes of the powerful, and yet sometimes, in a single sentence, it allows us to glimpse the cracks in their own story.

It is sobering to recognise that progressiveness offers no immunity from the structures that shape us. This is the inheritance I am still untangling. A longing to be close to the place my ancestors once called home but also occupied. I wonder if, in some way, he too had felt the fracture between the human and the imperial.

I thought again of that girl kneeling by the water, asking the land for its secrets. I cannot change the story that brought my ancestors here, but I can choose how I arrive. Not above, not outside, but with a willingness to see, to learn, to listen.

In truth, it wasn't the first time I had tried to belong to this land. I don't remember when the lie started, only that it gave me something to hold, a story that shimmered with spice and mystery. During my childhood my grandmother still travelled back to India most years to visit her guru and the only home she'd known until her early teens. She would return with gifts made of peacock feathers and gold glitter.

When I told my classmates I was half Indian, it didn't feel like deceit. It was a longing to claim an ancestry I thought in part was mine. But one day a girl at school looked at me with the blunt certainty only children possess and said, *"You can't be Indian, you're not brown."* I remember the bewilderment more than the hurt. I had not yet learnt that skin came with borders, or that identity could be something others felt entitled to approve or deny.

Looking back, I can see that this unknowing was not just innocence, but an inheritance. Privilege shows itself not only in what you have, but in what you have the luxury not to see. The stories you are spared from carrying, the truths you are permitted to overlook.

I had moved through my life believing the empire's story belonged to another era, another family, another kind of person, certainly not to me. This blindness, like a soft cushion passed down through generations, allowed me to drift above the darker truths that shaped the world beneath my feet. The ability to ignore history, to have no need to interrogate the soil my life grew from, is itself a kind of power.

I have been allowed to visit racism like a room with a door I could close when the truth grew too heavy. A place I could step into, study, and step back out of when it became too uncomfortable.

Whilst for others I now see, it's the air they are forced to breathe, the weather they must endure with no shelter from the storm. Their bodies read long before their names are known.

That night, between the whirr of the fan and the slow breathing of the river beyond the walls, I felt the lie loosen its grip. The lie that I stood outside this history, untouched by its shadow. The empire's story had travelled farther than ships and borders. It had travelled into language, into posture, into the silences I had learned to keep.

I could no longer pretend the story belonged to someone else. It lived in my voice, my comfort, my capacity to leave.

YOGA

Wow. What a word. Worn by time, changed almost beyond recognition, like sea glass shaped by a thousand restless waves, yet still holding the tender truth of its earliest form.

It has crossed continents, languages, and centuries, gathering an almost cult-like following in its wake. The word shimmers with promise. It has been stretched, repackaged, sold, worshipped, and adorned. Paired with everything from goat classes to corporate retreats, marketed as fitness, therapy, lifestyle, and salvation. It is loved and cherished, misunderstood and commodified, a word to live by and a word to profit from.

Perhaps it is no surprise that so much has

happened to a word whose Sanskrit root, *yuj*, means to unite, to join, to bring together. It signifies union, and in a deeper sense the merging of the individual self *(jīvātman)* with the universal consciousness *(paramātman)*.

Our *Haṭha Yoga* teacher, Mohanji, at the Nāda Yoga School, would smile whenever someone asked what he thought of all the different types of yoga. *"All yoga is good yoga,"* he would say, his voice calm, certain and laced with gentle affection.

Yoga at its essence is about integration, of body and breath, of self and world, of inner and outer life. And so, even in its fragmented modern forms, it is still doing its work, pulling opposites toward each other, creating conversation and connecting people.

If we are to truly practise yoga, we cannot begin by creating division. To argue over good yoga and bad yoga, authentic and diluted, Eastern and Western, is already to step away from its essence. The moment we draw those lines, we forget what the word itself has been trying to teach us, that wholeness cannot be built on separation. Yoga asks us to dissolve the boundaries, not reinforce them.

I was born into a world that worships analysis. Raised on debate, critical thinking, and the habit of sorting ideas into hierarchies of right and wrong. I was surprised at how easily I accepted Mohanji's simple, yet powerful, response. There was no need to debate, no hierarchy to climb, no winner to be crowned. Just a simple faith in the essence of the yoga itself.

Later, I came to understand it wasn't the phrase that carried power but the person who spoke it. Mohanji had studied yoga for years, committed to the discipline and precision of his practice, yet he held no arrogance about form. He bore no resentment toward those who taught yoga differently, no impulse to protect ownership of the word. His belief was not naïve; it was spacious. It came from a place where certainty softens into wisdom, and knowledge no longer needs to compete to prove itself.

This is not to say I do not believe in the richness that comes from studying the deeper essence of yoga, or from learning the meaning of the Sanskrit words woven through its philosophy. There is much to be gained from that journey. But it is not to be held up as virtuous or used as proof of one's worth over another. The moment we do that, we are using yoga to reinforce the very walls it was designed to dismantle.

Before I arrived in Rishikesh, I had never really paused to question what the word *āsana* truly meant. In the studios of London and Singapore, it was simply shorthand for the postures. We moved through choreographed sequences of stretch and strength on polished floors, beneath soft lighting and carefully curated playlists. I hurried from one class to the next, squeezing practice between chores and obligations, chasing flexibility and control. I pushed deeper into postures because the teacher said so, because effort was worthy, because endurance felt like an achievement.

Mohanji guided us to trace the word back to its Sanskrit root, *ās*, meaning to sit, not to sweat, not to sculpt, not to contort into ever more elaborate geometry. Just to sit. This gentle command had been whispered through the practice of yoga for thousands of years. Āsana, for all its beauty, was never the end point, only a preparation into something deeper.

In the *Yoga Sūtras*, Patanjali dedicates only one line to it: *"sthira sukham āsanam",* translating roughly to a posture that is steady and comfortable. *How could something so simple feel so confronting?* Its original pulse was not movement at all, but the ability to remain still. The body, for all its ancient wisdom, is a restless animal. And although the posture of sitting may appear simple, stillness is not.

It's not a state that I, or most people, could simply slip into on command. Stillness does not come when summoned like a well-trained servant. The body, so accustomed to motion as proof of purpose, muscles twitch with half-forgotten urgencies. The mind, startled by the absence of noise, rummages through memories, to-do lists and old wounds. To be still is to be exposed. To remain seated is to sit with everything you feel.

Mohanji treated āsana not as a routine of postures but as a conversation with the nervous system. We practised every morning as the mountains exhaled their cool breath across the Ganga. I unrolled my mat in the same place each day, more out of habit than attachment.

At first I shivered, the mat faintly damp with morning dew, but soon the heat rose from within. Mohanji asked us not how far we could stretch, but where the body wanted to retreat. Which muscles clenched before the stretch arrived. Which thoughts rushed in to override sensation.

Breath by breath, posture by posture, my body revealed itself. Evolving slowly, like a hesitant confession. Some days it felt like a shoreline holding last night's storm. Other days the tide had finally gone out, leaving room to breathe. Each pose became an invitation rather than a trophy to achieve.

Mohanji would remind us that āsana is one thread of the tapestry. A flexible body can still house a turbulent mind. Strength in the limbs does not guarantee steadiness in the heart. Yoga asks not just for movement, but for integration.

Without the breath to anchor us, without self-study to illuminate our patterns, without stillness to digest what rises, the postures remain exercise. It is the inner orientation that transforms stretching into practice, effort into presence, and movement into a doorway to the Self.

Resmaa Menakem writes in *My Grandmother's Hands* about how our bodies carry survival strategies inherited across generations. As reflexes of a nervous system trained over centuries to prioritise safety through distance and control. A jaw that tenses, a breath that rises and stays high in the chest, a spine that stiffens at the slightest hint of vulnerability.

I have learnt this in my own jaw, seeing it respond to an imagined threat. During a season of life when worry lived permanently behind my eyes, my body began to brace itself even in sleep. Night after night I clenched my teeth with such force that, by morning, my mouth barely opened at all. Eating became laboured. I searched for a medical fix, but there was nothing structurally wrong. Finally, a doctor said, almost casually, *"you need to be less stressed."*

It felt absurdly simple, and impossibly hard. Yet my body had already delivered the diagnosis my mind refused to hear. The tension I could not name in waking life had found its voice whilst I slept. It was my first undeniable lesson that the mind does not merely inhabit the body, it speaks through it, shapes it, and, when unheard, can bind it.

The morning āsana practices with Mohanji began to unwind the stories of tension my body held. My breath dropped lower into my belly. Some days it happened only for a breath or two, like catching sight of an animal before it darts back into the trees. But even in those fleeting moments, I felt something shift, a loosening and with it a sense of peace.

I was no longer using my body as something to conquer or perfect. I was learning to listen to it. To honour its fatigue rather than override it. Somewhere between the chanting, the stillness, and the slow unfolding of each posture, my relationship with my body began to soften. It stopped being a project and started becoming a companion.

I found gratitude for this body, not for how it looked, but for how faithfully it had carried me. For the memories it held, the warnings it sent, the resilience it showed even when I treated it like an obstacle. I began to see my body as the home of my soul, not a problem to be fixed, but a place to return to. A place that had always been mine, waiting for me to arrive with presence rather than judgement.

As this softness grew, something else rose to the surface. An awareness of the conditioning I had absorbed over time about what it means to inhabit a female body. I had been taught, like so many women, to fear aging, to brace for the slow fade into the background, to expect invisibility as the natural inheritance of womanhood. And yet, here I was, beginning to feel more alive in my body than ever before. Not as an ornament, but as a living, sensing, expressive home.

There was a new kind of presence growing in me, not the kind that needed admiration, but the kind that rooted me into myself. Here the thought came to me, maybe aging wasn't a diminishing after all, but an arrival, a deepening into a different kind of radiance.

In our group was living proof of that possibility. Gea van Dijk, a tall, radiant Dutch woman who lived in Nairobi. She was the oldest in the group, but she carried glamour like a second skin, luminous without effort or apology. I watched her with a kind of hunger, hoping to learn the secret alchemy that allowed her to inhabit herself so generously.

Over cups of chai one afternoon, she told me her ritual was a single headstand every morning to keep her energy young. I hadn't yet mastered the pose, but the next day in our Haṭha Yoga class with Mohanji, I felt a new determination to turn my world upside down, if only to see what fresh perspective might come into view.

I began to understand that the disconnect I felt from my body, the one that seemed to widen with age, wasn't personal failure; it was inherited conditioning. So much of my self-criticism had never belonged to me. It was the sum of comments, expectations, and unspoken rules about what a woman should be.

In that yoga hall, surrounded by women shedding the same inherited scripts, I realised how deeply I had internalised the impossible demand to be the *"ideal woman"*. Dr Jessica Taylor writes in her book *Sexy But Psycho* that this ideal has barely shifted for centuries, and that any deviation from it was once grounds to medicate, institutionalise, or even kill women under the guise of witchcraft. Our inherited conditioning has handed us survival patterns. We incarcerate ourselves for a war that's fought in the name of someone else's peace.

Through this lens, even Gea's headstand ritual took on a different meaning. It wasn't about defying age or chasing youth; it was an embodied refusal to disappear. A declaration of aliveness in a world that so often silences older women. Watching her,

I realised that reclaiming the body is not just a spiritual practice but a radical act of self-definition.

Each time I showed up on my mat, each time I breathed into tension instead of bracing against it, I was rewriting something in myself. I was no longer sculpting myself into the woman the world wanted. I was returning to the woman I had been before the world draped her in shame. Every posture became a small rebellion, a quiet undoing. A reminder that my body had never been the enemy.

On those mornings, I finally understood the kind of union yoga had been whispering all along. Not a grand merging of ideas, but the slow, patient stitching together of the parts of myself I had sent into exile. There was no trumpet call, no sudden clarity. Only the steady, forgiving rhythm of the breath. And in that steady return, I felt myself hovering between maps, the one I had inherited and the one I was only just beginning to draw.

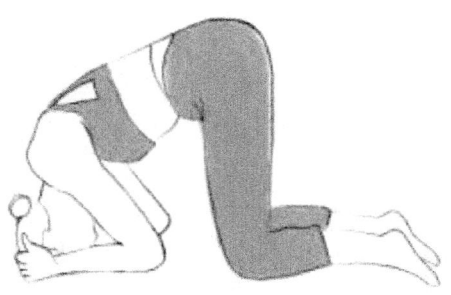

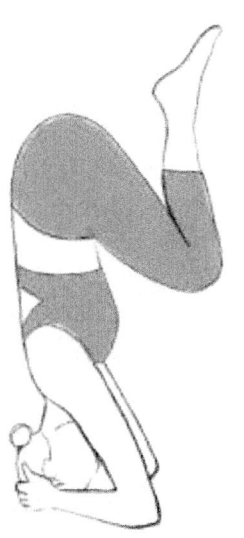

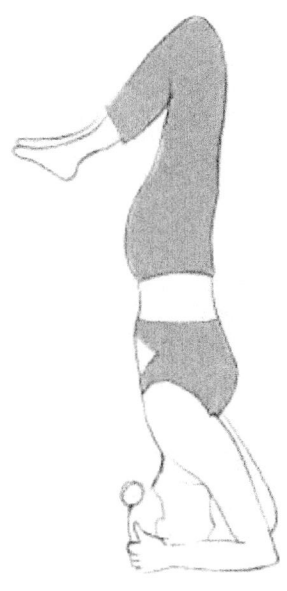

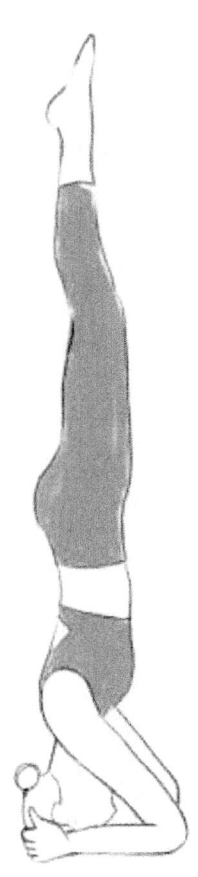

SAVIOUR

I grew up believing that helping others was simple. Those who have, give and those who lack, receive. As a child, I had been on the receiving end on many occasions. My first portal to the world of the internet arrived through a charity that refurbished old bank computers, to ease what was then coined *"digital poverty"*.

As I grew older, a new kind of exchange began to appear. A narrative in which the giver is cast as benevolent, enlightened, even righteous. A familiar glow of the empire's story. Providing a comforting illusion of innocence while obscuring the histories that made such inequalities possible in the first place.

It invites us to believe that all generosity is virtuous, no matter the impact on those who receive it. It frees us from asking the harder questions. And when charity becomes a stage with the giver cast as the hero, even good intentions crystallise into a kind of self-absolution, haloed and exempt from examination.

White saviourism often announces itself in grand, photogenic gestures, the kind that look noble from a distance but unravel under closer scrutiny. A library built in a village where few people can read. Donations that flood a local market and erode the livelihoods of the people they were meant to support. The volunteer who arrives with enthusiasm and departs with photographs, affording more benefit to their image than to the community they intended to serve.

These acts gleam with generosity but are shaped by assumptions. That our resources, our ideas, our conviction must surely be the solution. In this way, harm slips in through the back door, carried by the very hands that believe they are helping.

The same conditioning appears in quieter, almost invisible ways. In how we take up too much room in a conversation, mistaking our own vantage point for the universal view. In the moral sword we lift so readily, always aimed outwards. It surfaces in our instinct to explain rather than listen, to correct rather than ask, to assume leadership even when we have no knowledge of the terrain.

These habits do not make headlines, but they leave their mark all the same. They reveal how easily good intentions become a performance of righteousness, one that shields us from examining our own participation in the systems we claim to oppose.

At the Nāda Yoga School, up until this day, all of our teachers on our course had been men. When Joshita Arora arrived, it felt as though a new current of air had arrived with her. A young woman from Delhi, she carried a calm and contemplative energy. Her voice was soft but sure, each word measured. She spoke with the authority of someone who had wrestled with her own questions long before standing at the front of a class.

She guided us beyond the simple cause-and-effect definition of karma. Describing how the choices we make, the way we respond to others and the quality of our thoughts, each becomes a seed. And sooner or later, everything we plant blooms.

As the discussion deepened, the subject shifted toward the longer arc of karma, the idea that our current life is only one chapter in a much older story. She suggested that not everything we experience can be traced to this lifetime alone. Yoga philosophy suggests that relationships, fears, talents, and even illnesses may carry the scent of past lives, like unfinished threads seeking resolution.

My mind leapt to places outside of the conversation. I immediately asked how this teaching could possibly account for illnesses such as AIDS? I found myself climbing onto a soapbox, my voice tightening as conviction took over. I spoke of how dangerously convenient such beliefs could become, how history had shown us, time and time again, the harm caused when suffering was moralised or attributed to personal fault. *How many people had been shamed, ostracised, or blamed for their pain under the guise of karma or sin or destiny?*

As the words left my mouth, something strange happened. It was as though I briefly stepped outside of myself and saw the scene from above. Not the virtuous defender of justice I imagined I was, but a woman who had turned a gentle classroom inquiry into a battlefield of ideas, appointing herself the saviour of the oppressed when no one in the room had asked to be saved. I had come here to learn, yet with startling arrogance had slipped into the role of teacher, swinging my convictions like a sword rather than offering them as an exchange.

I have always believed in speaking up, in affirmative action and challenging harm where I see it. But in that moment I could hear the true motives beneath my words, the self-importance stitched into them, the subtle performance of righteousness. There was no injustice emerging, only a philosophical discussion that I had turned into a crusade.

Halfway through my monologue, the realisation caught in my throat. I stopped mid-sentence, and felt heat flood my cheeks. My mind raced with uncomfortable clarity. How many times had I let my ego bloom unchecked, dressed in the costume of moral duty, at the expense of someone else's dignity in a space we were meant to share?

In truth, karma isn't framed as blame or punishment, but as continuity. The soul's way of returning to whatever still needs to be understood, loved or healed. Rather than a cosmic scorecard, it is an unfinished conversation between lifetimes. Threads left loose that we are given another chance to weave into wholeness.

And yet, even with all this reflection, I must confess, I still find the notion of karma hard to swallow. There are moments when it feels too neat, too tenderly wrapped, too celestial a bow tied around the brutal edges of reality.

Nowhere do I feel this more strongly than in the stories of refugees. Perhaps this sensitivity is braided into my own lineage. The knowledge my own family had once escaped war, carrying only what could be grasped in trembling hands.

Yes, they were evacuated, and yes, their trauma was real, but the path carved for them was still padded by the privilege of empire, a privilege that shielded them from the kind of displacement I would later witness in the refugee camps born out of a different place in the world. The gulf between their experience and the desperation I saw years later was vast. Two worlds torn apart by war yet separated by an ocean of race, power, and history.

Some suffering does not arrive with poetic symmetry. Before I left for Singapore, I travelled with Emma and our friend Johanna to volunteer in the refugee camp in Calais, known as the Jungle. Words sometimes have a way of tidying what should remain unbearable, smoothing human suffering into something dangerously close to metaphor. In the word jungle, people were made into a landscape, their suffering absorbed into a name that incited imagination instead of accountability.

Emma and Johanna were working as nurses at the time and had signed up with a grassroots charity providing healthcare for low acuity illnesses, to relieve some of the pressure on Médecins Sans Frontières. With no medical qualifications then, I joined as an extra pair of hands. The operation was run out of a small, weather-beaten caravan in the middle of the camp.

I had travelled a fair bit by that point, including an internship in Bangladesh, so I knew poverty existed on a scale far beyond anything I had seen growing up on a council estate in South London. Still, my mind struggled to compute the contradiction before me. On the edge of an otherwise unremarkable French town, a country of châteaux, flowing wine, and weekend markets, stood a makeshift city of people who had lost everything except the will to keep moving.

The refugee camp echoed the early settlements along ancient trade routes, a sight until now I had only seen in history books and museums. A place born not of belonging but of movement and necessity. People from different nations building temporary homes side by side, each bringing fragments of their culture with them. You could see it in the way the camp was arranged. Those from industrialised cities had set up small shops, barber tents, even makeshift restaurants, recreating what they once knew of community and survival.

Then there were the boys, so young, most of them from Sudan, from rural villages scarred by genocide and ethnic cleansing. They did not have the same structure to fall back on. They sat together in tight clusters, as if proximity alone could offer protection, huddled around campfires, shoes worn by the journeys they had taken.

I began to notice that some of the people who queued for our small clinic were not physically sick at all. Alongside plasters and paracetamol, what we were really offering was reassurance and a friendly voice. And there was an appetite for that.

Many had endured persecution so severe it had hollowed them out, and the hostility didn't end when they reached Europe. People are often wary of those who arrive with nothing. The kind hand to the weary traveller that exists in fairy tales rarely presents itself at the borders of a nation.

One man's story has stayed with me ever since. John, not his birth name I suspect, but the name he chose to meet me with that day. He came from Sudan; his left arm amputated above the elbow.

He had just arrived at the camp, having walked from Paris. Only later did I realise that journey would have been around 200 miles. Now, whenever I see organised charity walks, bright banners, sponsorship pages, crowds cheering, I think of him. No supporters. No medals. No fundraising. Just sheer necessity, and the will to stay alive.

He told me he was waiting for the outcome of his asylum claim and had been advised it would take at least three months. He didn't believe he would survive on the streets of Paris for that long, so he walked to Calais, having heard rumours that in the Jungle there was food, shelter, and perhaps safety.

When I asked what medical attention he needed, he showed me the scars from bullet wounds on his legs and chest. There was nothing to treat: no infection, no bleeding. The past had written itself onto his flesh, impossible to erase. I asked whether he was in pain, he said "no," with his eyes lowered to the floor.

After learning he had arrived with nothing, I offered to take him to the information tent where another charity was handing out tents and sleeping bags. We got there too late. A volunteer closing up apologised and told him to come back tomorrow.

John didn't plead, argue, or insist, as I perhaps would have in his place. He simply turned to me, smiled and said, *"Thank you, sister,"* before walking back into the camp as the night began to fall.

I stood there for a moment, feeling the distance between us, not measured in wealth or comfort, but in what we had learned to expect from the world. We were met with so much gratitude for doing so little in the Jungle.

None of us were equipped for the depth of

trauma staring back at us. I began to question myself. *What was I really bringing? Was this help or was it poverty tourism disguised as compassion?* Another strain of white-saviour heroism dressed up as goodwill.

Not long after returning from Calais, my mum invited me to an exhibition about refugees. It was called Palimpsest. I remember having to google the meaning of the word. It refers to a manuscript or piece of writing material that has been reused. Where the original text has been scraped or washed off so new text could be written over it, but traces of the old writing remained beneath the surface.

At the White Cube in Bermondsey, the names were written in water. They rose slowly from the stone floor, letter by letter, until they formed and faded again, leaving only a dark trace of damp behind. Each name belonged to someone who had drowned, men, women, children, those who had tried to cross the sea and never arrived.

The air in the gallery was heavy, the kind that insists that you hold your breath without meaning to. People moved quietly, their footsteps soft against the stone, as though sound itself might disturb the dead. I stood watching the names appear and disappear. The water seeped through the pores of the stone, like tears rising from the earth. My mouth was dry, my passport heavy in my pocket.

The stories were powerful and exquisitely displayed. I felt suspended somewhere between admiration for the attention given to the suffering and the discomfort that suffering itself had become something to be viewed, contemplated, and then neatly exited through the gift shop.

LOVE

It arrives in more shapes than language can describe. Threading itself through our lives. As parental love, fierce and strong. As friendships that feel like your chosen constellations. As the soft belonging of a community. As devotion to the world itself, to trees and oceans and the sky's changing moods. Not forgetting as lovers, the tender, volatile, transformative kind that happens in the space between two people, a space that can soften or sharpen us with equal force. It expands and shapeshifts, revealing itself sometimes in places we have forgotten to look.

As my relationship with myself softened, so too did the way I met others. Friendships formed easily, uncomplicated and generous. On the Nāda Yoga course I discovered how healing it can be to share space with others whose journeys reflect your own.

Sue was older than me, yet she held the irrepressible spirit of someone seeing life for the first time. She felt like sunlight in human form. Radiant, alive, and unmistakably Australian. I loved listening to stories of her adventures across India, sometimes with friends and sometimes alone. She told tales of adventure, jumping on trains between sacred cities, hopping on the back of strangers' motorbikes.

Sue rarely questioned the motives of the people she met along the way. She trusted the world in a way I did not. But I trusted her and during one of our breaks between classes, I found myself following Sue to a tattoo studio on the outskirts of Tapovan.

The day before, she had met a woman in a café who mentioned that her boyfriend was a tattoo artist. For Sue, this was not a coincidence but a sign. She had been carrying the desire for a Hamsa tattoo for years: a symbol of protection, a sacred palm crossing cultures and faiths, echoing her Jewish heritage and the spiritual path she had carved for herself.

In truth, the *'studio'* was less a studio and more a bedroom with a tattoo gun. The tattoo artist was a half-baked stoner who rescued stray dogs. I found a space to sit, careful not to disturb the dogs who had claimed most of the floor as their own. The walls were painted a fluorescent shade of green, and the bed was draped in a soft, furry animal print throw. The tattooist's seat was a plastic garden chair; it screamed of the unpolished fun I hadn't realised I'd been missing.

Sue settled onto the bed with natural ease, chatting to the artist as though they were old friends rather than two people who had met only moments before. I sat nearby, taking it all in. Watching how this was something she did effortlessly; she leaned into life without needing all the variables to line up first. She trusted moments as they arrived.

Before the sensibility of adulting tightened its grip, there had been a free-spirited teenager inside me, and I realised how long it had been since I'd let her breathe. On impulse, I reached into my bag for a pen and inscribed अनाहत नाद *(Anāhata Nāda)* onto my right wrist. The tattoo is not perfect; its lines are slightly uneven, its edges a little raw. And perhaps that is why I love it so much. It is a permanent reminder that life's truest magic is often found in the beautifully imperfect. An invitation to step beyond caution, towards happiness and the luminous thrill of having fun.

The idea that there might be something better beyond perfection had first come to me months earlier, in a Japanese temple. I stood watching the rain slide over rows of pristine green tiles, each one gleaming like polished jade. On the wall, a small plaque, the kind you might find in a gallery, caught my eye. It explained that one roof tile was always deliberately laid the wrong way round.

Perfection, it read, leaves no room for the divine and only through imperfection can the spirit enter. It was my first encounter with the Japanese philosophy of wabi-sabi, a reverence for what is incomplete and beautifully flawed.

Somewhere between Japan and Rishikesh, between the tiles and the mantras, I began to learn the art of letting go. The temple had offered the idea, and yoga had turned it into a practice. To see imperfection, impermanence, and incompleteness as beauty, is to see the world through an entirely different lens, one in which there is little to fix or improve.

As my *Nāda Yoga* teacher training drew to a close, we were each asked to prepare a final class, our offering and our initiation into becoming teachers. I wanted mine to reflect the raw, imperfect process of learning to show up as myself and I was searching for the words to verbalise such a shift.

For all its poetry, the English language so often falls short when asked to hold the subtle, the sacred, the ineffable. It leans toward definition, towards certainty, towards closure. Experiences of the inner world, those delicate tremors of awakening, intuition, déjà vu of the soul, require a different tongue. I began to understand why Sanskrit has travelled alongside spiritual practice for millennia. It is not just a language, but a frequency of consciousness. Each word feels less like a label and more like a doorway.

Anāhata was one word that gathered everything I had experienced and reflected it back to me. The literal Sanskrit translation is 'unstruck sound,' that which arises without two things hitting. It echoed the revolution that had unfurled in me; the willingness to loosen my grip on what was known and step beyond logic into the terrain of devotion, intuition, and invisible threads. It carried the feeling of being guided by something ancient and intimately familiar.

It is also associated with the heart chakra. Anāhata is the realm of love in its most spacious form. I felt my heart widen in those weeks, not in a way that diluted the love I held for those closest to me, but in a way that allowed it to overflow its old boundaries. Love became less of a possession and more of a state of being. A tenderness without transaction. It is the peace within when love is offered without reciprocity.

My final class was a ceremonial declaration of love to my group. I crafted it the way you might see in a romance film. I scattered petals across the floor, left cards inscribed with words of gratitude, and placed a small gift on each mat. I chose music that reminded me of them, knowing that one day, hearing those songs again would pull me back to this moment like a thread through time.

During the final meditation, an ethereal stillness settled over the room. They lay in *śavāsana* with their eyes closed and hands loosely woven together. I looked around at the circle they'd become. A constellation of souls who had arrived as strangers and now breathing as one. I drew in the moment with a deep breath and my body flooded with euphoria.

It often strikes me how astonishingly powerful our bodies are and how little we are taught about the inner pharmacy we carry. We grow up learning the names of external remedies, chocolate for comfort, wine to unwind, caffeine to cope, pills to sleep, pills to wake, pills to feel less, pills to feel more.

Yet we are taught little about the natural chemicals our bodies release when we breathe with intention, move with freedom, or connect with others. We are walking apothecaries of euphoria and calm, but we've forgotten how to unlock the cabinet.

Oxytocin, the molecule of bonding and trust, flows simply from holding hands and singing together. Serotonin rises with the feeling of belonging. Dopamine spikes with the tiny thrill of trying something new. Together, they remind us that so much of what we seek is already being brewed within us.

I couldn't help but wonder what might shift in our world if we were taught to generate our own joy before seeking it elsewhere. If we were shown that the body is not a machine to be managed but a garden to be tended. Capable of cultivating its own medicine when given the right conditions. In that moment, sitting in a circle, I tasted a kind of joy that was clean, potent, and entirely self-made.

It reminded me of something I'd first encountered years earlier in an economics lecture: the Paradox of Value. It describes a curious contradiction at the heart of our systems of worth, how the things essential to our survival, like water, are considered cheap, while things with little practical use, like diamonds, are valued beyond measure. This paradox would echo far beyond textbooks, quietly shaping how we learn to measure our own lives.

How easily we trade the essential for the ornamental. How subtly we learn to desire what dazzles rather than what nourishes. The paradox was never just an economic theory; it seeped into the architecture of our choices, our insecurities, and the stories we tell ourselves about what makes a life worthwhile.

One of the songs I played that day was *I Am What I Am* by Aykanna. I carried it back to my apartment in Singapore like a private note to myself.

On the flight home, I listened to it on repeat, the mantra looping through my headphones as the plane cut across continents. Somewhere over the Bay of Bengal, with the world reduced to a dark sky and a humming cabin, the words wrapped around me like a shawl. The kind a parent might drape over your shoulders without asking, holding me gently, tucking in the parts of me that felt exposed to the cold air of change.

I pressed my forehead to the window and watched the night below, anonymous cities, scattered lights, sleeping oceans, and I felt something inside me settling, rearranging the certainty into a gentler kind of knowing.

By the time the plane touched down, the mantra had stitched itself into me, like the ink on my wrist, not as a memory of India, but as a compass for what needed to come next. It laid the foundations for the conversation with Patrick, the one that would open the door to returning to London.

During that month in India, I had forgiven myself

for wanting to go home. We both knew moving home would not drain the ocean that had gathered between us, but returning was the first step toward building a bridge across it.

The move came quicker than expected, and by May we were back in blighty. It felt significant because May is my favourite month. Not only because it cradles my birthday, but because May feels like the year's first inhale, the moment the world remembers how to bloom again. The first of May has long been a whisper of new beginnings, when the old loosens its grip and something fresh dares to take root.

A spring shower had just rolled in. Patrick and I ran through the rain-kissed cobbled streets of Covent Garden, the stones beneath us shining like they had been newly polished. London felt like a city awakening under our feet. One of the things I had missed most about home, beyond the familiar faces and voices, was its architecture. Buildings that stood as storytellers beyond their structures.

I had learnt that Aykanna was going to be in London delivering a workshop called *The Song of the Heart: Creating Meaningful Relationships.* Patrick, always game for trying something new, agreed to give it a go, but I was unsure he truly knew what he was signing up for.

The Swiss Church sat on Endell Street. It was elegant in an understated way, with its white walls and sunlight filtering through tall windows, softening as it touched the polished wooden floor. There is a particular discomfort that Western bodies carry into spaces of intimacy, the emotional stiffness of people taught to keep their feelings neatly folded, like napkins at a formal dinner table.

At first, Patrick and I moved like visitors. We sat upright, polite, measuring the room with guarded smiles. When asked to breathe deeply, we inhaled like students trying to get the exercise *right*. When invited to look into each other's eyes, we did so awkwardly. The resistance was palpable, the impulse to analyse, to intellectualise, to stay dignified. But there was also curiosity, a longing beneath the surface.

As the workshop unravelled, we were invited into simple practices that felt strangely daring for a Sunday afternoon. We breathed together in synchrony, learning to share the same air. We spoke small truths, first in whispers, then with steadier voices. We placed a hand on each other's hearts, and felt the warmth, the vulnerability, and the unmistakable reminder of the living person beyond years of habit and routine.

Aykanna shared pieces of their own love story with a kind of gentle transparency that made the whole room soften. They spoke of partnership not as a fairytale, but as a practice, a devotion, a daily tuning of two souls learning how to stay awake to one another.

I thought of bell hooks' book *All About Love*, where she dismantles the myth that love just happens to us. She reminds us that love is not the soft blur of romance, but the discipline of seeing and being seen. In that room, I began to recognise how easily we confuse love with longing, and how different it feels when we treat love as a conscious choice rather than a state to fall into.

Choosing each other, I was learning, is not the same as clinging to each other. It asks for the courage to speak of endings while you are still inside the story. To name the fault lines before the ground gives way. There is a particular terror in admitting that love is struggling, because it threatens the myth that love should always be our saviour.

It was only when we approached the edges of existence, that something more honest became possible. We choose each other with conscious awareness, meeting each other exactly where we were. There is peace in knowing you have weathered a storm and not only survived but emerged stronger.

GURU

I think I was about seven when I asked my schoolteacher if he had a guru. He said no, with the calm authority of an adult who assumes that is the end of a conversation. Unfazed, I pressed on. *"Do you have Knowledge?"* This time he looked puzzled.

"What do you mean?" he said. I explained, with the absolute conviction only a child can muster, that if he didn't have *Knowledge* but wanted it, then he was an *Aspirant*. He smiled politely, perhaps thinking it was some playground invention.

How funny I thought, a teacher who didn't have *Knowledge*, or even seem to know what it was. I still carried the childhood belief that schoolteachers were walking encyclopaedias who knew everything.

Knowledge, in my world, wasn't an abstract idea; it was something you were given by your guru. You had to wait until you were an adult to get it, and my parents wouldn't tell me what it was, which both intrigued and annoyed me.

My family's guru is Prem Rawat, known to his followers as Maharaji. Those who follow Maharaji call themselves Premies, the name is drawn from *prem*, the Sanskrit word for love. My grandmother has spent much of her life traveling the world to be in his presence. Her devotion to him has outlasted seasons, fashions and marriages.

My mum only brushed against the idea of having a guru, and by the time I reached my teens, my dad had moved on to other things. What I carried were fragments of memory and the blurred remnants of a child's view.

There is something peculiar about childhood memories. They travel with us like sealed envelopes, carried unopened for years, until one ordinary day in adulthood they choose to unfold themselves.

During my stay at the Nāda Yoga School,

someone invited me to a *satsang (satsaṅga)* at the Parmarth Niketan Ashram. I recognised the word instantly. It had been resting somewhere in my vocabulary, half-forgotten, waiting for this very moment to reveal itself.

Hearing the word satsang that day pulled the pieces back into view. Suddenly I was back in the red-brick community hall. Chairs lined up in obedient rows, all facing the large screen. Maharaji appeared larger than life, seated and speaking directly into the camera. The VHS recordings flickered on the screen; the room dim and hushed like a small cinema.

I can still picture the coloured sound graph flickering like a tiny rainbow heartbeat at the bottom of the screen, and the long, heavy spaces he left between words. These memories are not wrapped in the joy of devotion but in the impatience of a child who wished he'd hurry up.

That night at the Parmarth Niketan Ashram, satsang was given by a disciple of the ashram's guru, Sadhvi Bhagawati Saraswati (known as Sadhviji). It was January, and in the evenings a thin mountain chill crept into the air. The kind that urges you to pull your sleeves over your hands and hold your limbs in close. We all piled into a small room with low ceilings, bamboo cladding, and clusters of plants that softened the light. The room settling around us like a cosy coat pocket.

We sat cross-legged, side by side. She sat at the front; the spotlight aimed in her direction. It washed her orange robes in a saffron glow, sharpening the edges of her eyes until they gleamed. Under that single, watchful beam, she looked momentarily borrowed from a myth.

Sadhviji was unmistakably an intellectual. Braiding neuroscience with the Vedas, psychology with prayer, as though each belonged to the same lineage of truth. And yet I found myself wondering how she had surrendered her life to something that is founded in faith of the unknown. She listened to each question put to her with rare attentiveness, responding with a clarity that felt both authentic and intuitively perceptive.

I was intrigued by this white woman who had given up everything, her home, her career, even her name, to live here permanently on the banks of the Ganga.

In Rishikesh, white faces are common, but most arrive chasing something transient. A retreat, a course, a transformation that can be neatly packaged back into their ordinary life. Few stay. Still fewer take vows of renunciation, of *sannyasa (sannyāsa),* exchanging comfort for devotion.

Yet Sadhviji had done exactly that. She had been living this way for decades, not as a spiritual experiment or an aesthetic choice, but as her life. There was no trace of performance in her presence. Just the peace in her eyes made me question, *what she had found here that was worth staying for?*

Not long after I returned to London, Sadhviji visited with her guru Pujya Swami Chidanand Saraswati, also known as Swamiji. The event, *Peace in the Chaos,* was held in a large hall in West London. Hundreds of people gathered as he spoke about the Gita's teaching and practices to return to inner stillness. The night unfolded in kirtan, and for one enchanting evening, it felt as if Rishikesh itself had crossed continents, settling for a few luminous hours in my hometown.

When it finished, I ached to return with them to the banks of the Ganga. There is a pulse to that river, ancient and alive, that seems to rise through your skin until you can no longer tell where your heartbeat ends and hers begins. In Rishikesh, it is easy to believe in the sacred; the mountains conspire to make you porous. But in my London apartment, I had to work harder to keep the embers alight.

Sadhviji's books had travelled back to London with me, still smelling faintly of ashram incense. I searched them for answers, longing to understand how she had let go. Her writing spoke to me. She didn't speak in declarations but acted like a guide. Gently drawing back the curtains rather than telling you where to look.

I had long believed that no matter how pure a guru's intentions might be, the very architecture of hierarchy and devotion forged a countdown to its own unravelling. As my adolescence took root, so did my conviction that gurus were for people who needed to be told what to think, and I wore my self-reliance like a badge of honour.

At university in a politics lecture, I listened with a keen ear to Lord Acton's warning about the moral hazards of concentrated authority, his sharp observation that *"Power tends to corrupt, and absolute power corrupts absolutely."* It had lodged itself in me like a compass point, shaping the way

I viewed anyone placed on a pedestal, however benevolent they appeared.

For a long time I had been wearing my critical mind like armour, seeing reason as freedom. But armour grows heavy after a while, and I was beginning to feel its weight.

In Sadhviji's book *Satsang*, she responds to questions about knowing the difference between a real guru and a fake one. Her answers are disarmingly simple. Guiding the reader to flee anyone who labours to convince you of their enlightenment and be wary of those who wrap everyday truths in unnecessary complexity. It made me laugh out loud. I read it like an auntie's no-nonsense pep talk. Imagining her whispering with a side glance, and telling me, *"If he needs to tell you he's a good man, he's not a good man."* Her tone cut through the mystique, reminding me that wisdom doesn't have to be solemn.

She also reminds the reader that if you are truly in the presence of an enlightened being, you won't need their proclamations; their very presence will soften you. You will not need words because you will feel peace, you will feel love.

Reading her words back in London, I couldn't

deny how fragile my own practice felt. The peace I had carried home from India was already slipping through my fingers, like trying to hold grains of sand. Each day it grew thinner, harder to grasp, dissolving into the familiar rhythm of alarms and expectations.

I read her words on crowded Tube trains, shoulder to shoulder with strangers, the city's impatience vibrating through the metal rails, most of us heading to our desks and deadlines. I wondered how such stillness could coexist with life here. Clutching a book about liberation while inching towards my civil-service cubicle. The fact that I had become the ultimate cliché was not lost on me, another city dweller hunting for transcendence between rush-hour stops.

A few months later, I was on a plane again. Rishikesh drawing me back into its loving embrace. This time I stayed at the Parmarth Niketan Ashram and enrolled on a beginner yoga course. Alongside the deepening of my yoga practice, I held another desire. I wanted to know whether this time, in this place of prayers and pilgrims, I might find a guru. Or perhaps more hopefully, a guru might find me.

A requirement of the course was to wear white,

loose-fitting clothes. I had arrived with nothing but my tight leggings and sports tops. It was time to let go of my city clothes and the city habits I clung to, so I wandered into the market in search of something softer.

Every stall shimmered, turmeric yellow, marigold orange, deep indigo, as though draped in a sea of rainbows. I shyly held up garments against my body trying to guess my size. Soon I realised that when you are buying clothes designed to let you move, you can drift between sizes with surprising ease. Such a contrast with the rigid, often punishing rituals of shopping back home. Where numbers felt like accusations.

Beneath the riot of colour and joy, a thread of judgement tugged at me. The word appropriation echoed in my mind. I slipped a simple cotton kurta over my clothes, the material was soft, hand-embroidered, and light enough to move with the wind. The fabric fell differently against my skin, gentler, more forgiving. When I looked up, the women in the market smiled at me, their hands reaching out to straighten the fabric. *"So beautiful,"* one said, her eyes kind.

The ease of admiration here in India was

seductive, a balm I wanted to sink into without asking why it came so freely. I wanted their affection to absolve me, to let me hide inside the comforting cocoon of wilful unknowing. So that it might silence the drumbeat of privilege pounding at the edges of my awareness.

Earlier that morning, a lady at the ashram had pressed a small red bindi to the space between my eyes and told me it would draw my attention inwards. Standing there looking in the mirror of the market shop, it felt like my North Star, pointing me within.

Something in me responded, my mind's eye expanding perhaps, able to trace the legacy of an empire lingering in the small gestures. A request for a photo, a curious smile, a warmth that bordered on devotion. Not with guilt or defensiveness, but with a sharper, steadier awareness. I began to understand why people choose to wear symbols of faith, not as costume but as orientation points. Anchoring the mind in the sea of modern life.

The bindi started its life as bindu, meaning 'seed-dot'. In the Vedic imagination, this was the primordial point of creation, the seed from which sound, form, and the universe itself emerged. Travelling through centuries and collecting stories along the way. Slowly evolving into a dot to be worn. The red bindi is a tiny universe of meaning. In the colour lives the fierce vitality that is Shakti (Śakti). Resting on the third eye as a reminder to see more clearly, to live more consciously and honour the fire within.

Our yoga course was run by Induji. She had been teaching at the ashram for more than a decade, and yet she carried the lightness of someone newly in love with her own practice. Her eyes held a kindness that saw beneath the surface of a person. She could look into your eyes and see the script of your soul. With a tilt of her head or a gentle nod, she could draw the mantra from your throat as if she were coaxing a shy bird from its nest.

During one of our classes, I finally asked her the question that had been circling me for days. *How does one come to have a guru?* The words felt naïve as they left my mouth, but she received them with the same gentleness she brought to everything. She didn't answer immediately. Instead, she let the silence settle between us, then said gently, *"When you are ready, the guru will appear."*

That evening we were led to *darshan (darśana)* with Swamiji, the ashram's spiritual head and resident guru. The room was already filling up when we arrived. I watched Swamiji, with his saffron robes and kind eyes, addressing the crowd.

Around us, devotees folded their hands with practiced reverence, their faces lifted toward him, eyes bright, as though simply being in his presence brought them a kind of joy. I tried to imagine what it would take to bow to another human, to hand over that much trust.

Something within me began to stir, but not the deep sense of peace I was hoping for. The solemnity of it all, the slow choreography of bows and blessings, triggered that familiar feeling of giggles bubbling up inside. While the adults around me sank deeper into devotion, the child in me was watching the ceremony, like I was back in the community hall watching the sound-bar graph, complaining about how long it was until dinner.

I tried to anchor myself in the moment, but the mischievousness kept rising. She whispered her own running commentary in my ear, utterly unfazed by the fact that I was trying, somewhat desperately, to become holy.

My inner child reached her peak a moment later. As Swamiji approached, hand raised in blessing, my arm seemed to move of its own accord, lifting my hand with absolute accuracy to connect with his. He looked bemused, but not remotely rattled, and simply glided on to the next devotee as though high-fiving the guru was an entirely acceptable form of reverence. I sensed my initiation into higher wisdom would not be happening that day.

On the winding road of my spiritual path, I often turned to Bhuwanji whenever I felt adrift. A pragmatist with a steady faith and a disciplined practice, he had a way of offering clarity with just a few well-placed words. I began, as I always did, with my usual tumble of questions, *what does any of this mean? What's the point of having a guru?* He received my childlike *whys* with unshakeable calm, never irritated, only gently amused by the restless workings of my mind.

When I got myself so tied up on the topic, as something that needed to be completed, and moved on from, I eventually said, *"Can't you just be my guru?"* He just smiled and said, *"I'm not a guru.*"

I thought about how in his place I might have been offended. There I was, hoping to complete the task of '*having a guru*,' bypassing all the philosophical depth, craving only the tick in the box, a shortcut to spiritual achievement. It could easily have looked like I was making a mockery of liberation itself.

What I discovered slowly and almost reluctantly was that my suspicion of the guru was only half the story. The other was a bit more uncomfortable to face. Beneath my critiques, the political analysis, the philosophical arguments, the instinctive recoil from hierarchy, lived a quieter truth.

I wanted a guru. Not a person, nor a devotion, but the idea of one. A fantasy of certainty. A promise of arrival. A shortcut to salvation. There was corruption in my own desires. I wanted the symbol, the sheen of belonging, the illusion of depth without the real work of surrender. I wanted a spiritual inheritance without spiritual maturity. My longing was not rooted in readiness; it was rooted in acquisition.

Realising this was like being forced to look in a mirror I had been avoiding. But my yoga practice had been reshaping my sense of self, and I met this truth with tenderness rather than judgement. Yoga asked me to drop the fantasy of who I thought I should be and return to who I actually am. It taught me that there is no enlightenment waiting to be handed down from a pedestal; there is only the slow, steady willingness to sit with oneself.

I did not find a guru. I found something far less romantic and far more truthful. A capacity to meet myself exactly where I am, without shame. A willingness to stay with my own contradictions. An acceptance of the parts of me that still ache for certainty, even as I learn to stand without it.

I discovered that the only guru I was ready for was the one I had spent years overlooking: me. The part of me that pays attention, that listens inward, that refuses to abandon myself. And for the first time, I could offer that part of me something like devotion, not blind, not dependent, but wholehearted. Yoga did not give me a master; it gave me back myself.

SEVEN

After seven years away, I found myself back in Rishikesh for seven days. Seven is a number that appears like a secret reference in the world's oldest stories.

- 7 heavens
- 7 days of creation
- 7 seas
- 7 colours in a rainbow
- 7 chakras

Seven feels like the number of renewal, a cycle through which something completes itself only to begin again. I wanted to believe that I, too, had completed a cycle, that the person who had once come to Rishikesh in search of transformation had been remade.

I had once been told that the human body renews itself entirely every seven years. That by the time seven summers have passed, not one molecule of who you were remains. I liked that idea. It carried a promise that change is not only possible but inevitable.

However, science, as it often does, tells a more complicated truth. Our bodies do not, in fact, start afresh every seven years. Skin cells renew in weeks, red blood cells in months, bones in decades, and some brain cells never at all. We are not reborn every seven years; we are a mosaic of old and new, a living patchwork of what endures and what is replaced.

I can't help but think that myths endure because they speak to something deeper than fact. Perhaps the myth of seven-year renewal persists not for its accuracy, but because it offers language to a truth we feel but struggle to name. Maybe metaphors are the placebos our minds require. The stories we tell ourselves to make sense of the world and our existence. Could it be that science explains how we change, but metaphor gives us a way to feel it.

In yoga, mythology is not dismissed as fantasy

Seven

but revered as a language of truth spoken in symbols. The seven chakras, the seven stages of awakening, are not literal maps of the body, but mirrors of the spirit. Through them, we remember that transformation is both physical and unseen. The intangible measurable in neither years nor cells, but in the subtle tuning of our consciousness.

At our base, the **muladhara (mulādhāra)**, our root chakra, reminds us to ground ourselves and belong to the earth.

Svadhisthana (svādhiṣṭhāna), the sacral chakra, teaches us to feel, to let creativity and desire flow without shame.

In **manipura (maṇipūra)**, the solar plexus, we find our will, the fire to act and the courage to be.

As the energy rises to **anahata (anāhata)**, the heart chakra. We learn the alchemy of compassion, where pain transforms into empathy, and love becomes expansion.

When **vishuddha (viśuddha)** the throat chakra is

in balance, we communicate authentically with the courage to speak our deepest truths.

Through **ajna** (**ajñā**), our third eye, we awaken our perception beyond sight. This is where our intuition and inner wisdom reside.

And finally, **sahasrara** (**sahasrāra**), the crown chakra. Dissolving the illusion of separation, where the self unites with the infinite.

I returned to Rishikesh the way one returns to an ex, hesitant, guarded, half afraid of what I might find. I stepped out of the taxi and to my relief, so much of it still felt familiar. The ashram lands along the Ganga near Ram Jhula bridge remained spared from development, held in trust by the spiritual institutions, a barrier against the creeping concrete. This portion of the riverbank, sacred and slow, seemed to have kept its memory intact. Standing on the bridge, I watched the Ganga flow, eternal, indifferent and unchanged.

Walking back through the gates of the Parmarth Niketan Ashram felt like stepping into a memory that had been waiting patiently for me to return.

Seven

The same dusty pink walls, the same archway framing the hills behind, the faint scent of incense and sandalwood carried on the breeze from the market. The familiar soundscape, the echo of bells, birds calling from the ficus trees and the low hum of chanting. It was comforting, like slipping into an old pair of slippers still moulded to the shape of my feet.

So many memories lived here. Everything about the ashram seemed suspended in its own time, unchanged because it never pretended to keep pace with the world outside.

Parmarth, one of Rishikesh's largest and oldest ashrams, still held its steady rhythm of prayer, seva (sevā), and silence, anchored by the faith of its community. The faces behind the check-in desk were familiar, a little older perhaps, but with the same warmth in their eyes.

For a moment I thought they recognised me too. But then I saw it, their smiles were not memories, but practice. An unconditional welcome offered to every pilgrim who crossed that threshold. Part of me ached to be known. To be remembered. To be special.

The room I'd be given was always a mystery until

I arrived. I'd cross my fingers for one of the older ones with thick stone walls, small windows, and a whisper of time in every corner. There is something about the older buildings that gives a different energy. You can feel the past in the air; the memory of prayers and meditations still held in the walls.

Recent studies have shown that chanting and meditative practice alter brain-wave frequencies in lasting ways. When I sleep in one of these rooms, I feel like I am bathing in the vibrations of the past. And even if that sounds poetic, I find it plausible. *If the brain can shift with sound and time, why not space too?*

I had signed up for a seven-day *ShantiLotus Healing Dance* retreat. Our teacher met us at the reception. Her name was Tara Maa. A vibrant soul from Canada, with Indian roots and a hint of Caribbean rhythm from her childhood in Trinidad. Something of that island light seemed to travel with her, bright and warm.

Standing beside her was Uma, who was engaged in seva (sevā) at the ashram and assisting with the course. She carried a sweet, almost childlike energy, yet there was something

Seven

deeply maternal about her too. When I first encountered the practice of seva (sevā), it filled me with suspicion. A practice of giving one's time and effort without expectation of return, allowing service itself to become the teacher. It felt like a convenient set up for the receiver. But they were not captives, and even if devotion was what kept them here, I saw how it rearranged their sense of worth, offering a value that stretched far beyond financial gain.

It was Uma's task to guide us through the ashram. I had walked these paths many times before, yet this place never stopped revealing itself. Each visit felt like being re-introduced to someone you already loved, familiar, but never the same.

As we moved between courtyards, she told us about her family's long connection to the ashram. Her grandmother, she said, had bought an apartment on the grounds when it was first built in 1942. Although Uma had grown up in America, her family would spend their summers here, returning like migratory birds to the river's edge.

"It was different then," she said, smiling at a memory that seemed to belong to several

generations at once. *"There was chanting from morning till night, and not a single tourist in sight."* She spoke not with nostalgia that scorns the present, but with the tenderness of someone honouring what came before.

Our retreat followed a daily rhythm of breathwork, *mudra (mudrā),* mantra, dancing, and satsang led by Tara Maa. Alongside this, we were invited to join the ashram's own daily practices of yoga, *puja (pūjā),* arti (ārtī), darsan (darśan), and satsang with Swamiji and Sadhviji. An interlacing of movement, devotion, and stillness that shaped the cadence of each day.

During the dancing, Tara Maa weaved between us, her presence a steady tide. She didn't correct or reshape us. She held the space and gave us permission to let go. To unravel, to feel, to let the body lead the way. By the time the first session came to a close, we were no longer a room full of strangers. Each of us had walked a few steps closer to ourselves, and in doing so, closer to each other. After the final song, Tara Maa invited us to sit again in the circle. *"This is where the healing begins,"* she said, *"when you allow yourself to feel."*

During satsang that morning, we discussed the

topic of ego. Sometimes I have wondered if my longing to *'let go of the ego'* was just another performance of the ego itself, another scene in which I get to imagine I am more evolved than I really am.

My ego has always been there, humming in the background like an old generator, powering my need to be useful. To be seen as kind. To be the version of myself that deserves the approval. It would be dishonest to pretend that doing good has never been intertwined with wanting to feel good about who I am.

And yet, I can't dismiss the ego entirely. It has carried me through storms I might not have survived otherwise. It's pushed me to show up for people, to take responsibility, to try harder. It's easy to demonise it, to imagine it as a greedy little tyrant inside me, but sometimes it has simply been the part of me that refused to look away. The part that wanted to believe I could matter.

Tara Maa taught us that the problem isn't that the ego exists, but rather it's when it becomes the puppeteer instead of the witness. I felt this resonate, a place where the ego could live but needed a conscious eye. She described the ego as a child that needs attention and, when it is allowed to be seen, it folds itself into the background.

Nowhere do I encounter this more clearly than in my work on the ambulance. My ego is what leads me into the chaos, insisting I can rescue those in need. But it is the human connection that delivers the care.

I remember my first shift, my first patient, with the kind of clarity as though it happened only this morning. The call came in as a young man with breathing problems. On arrival we found him curled up like a fetus in bed, eyes wide and fixed, hands like ridged claws, shallow breaths rapidly spitting in and out of him. I sat down and placed my hand on his, introducing myself. I tried to guide him through the breathing technique we are taught for patients who are hyperventilating as a result of a severe panic attack.

Nothing in him acknowledged my presence, eyes still fixed. Desperate to find connection with him, I looked around and noticed he had a tattoo written in Hindi. I could read the *Devanagari* letters from my time spent learning Sanskrit, but rarely did I say them out loud. My ego relinquished, and like a child sounding out phonics for the first time, I mouthed the letters.

The shock of this blonde, white girl, in a green uniform speaking fractured Hindi was enough to pull him out of the anxiety vortex he had fallen into. His eyes caught mine long enough for me to help guide his consciousness back into the room. As his breathing returned to a steady rate and the excess carbon dioxide left his body, his hands softened. Within minutes he was sitting up in bed, chatting as if nothing had happened.

We had a break from classes in the afternoon, and I planned to visit the Nāda Yoga School, only a short walk from the ashram. I set off down the cobbled street, its stones worn smooth by pilgrims and time. The scent of chai, marigolds, and wood smoke drifted through the air, everything both changed and exactly the same. My feet knew the way before my mind caught up.

I had messaged Bhuwanji ahead of time, so he knew I was coming. But I hadn't reached out to Mohanji or the boys, and part of me doubted they'd recall my face among the many that had passed through. I was just another one of the carousel of white girls who had come to the Nāda Yoga School chasing transformation, leaving behind fragments of longing like offerings no one asked for.

When I arrived, the boys, Mohan and Rohit, were hardly recognisable themselves. Time was most visible on them, now standing before me as men. Their recognition stirred something in me I hadn't expected. I realised how much I had needed to be remembered, to be seen. Was it vanity or something more tender? I couldn't quite tell.

My ego burned quietly beneath the joy, whispering that my time here had meant something, that I had not simply been another passing seeker. There was sincerity too, a longing to belong not as a visitor, but as part of the fabric of this place, however small the thread. For all my talk of transformation and surrender, what I still craved was proof that I had mattered, that my presence had left a trace.

Recognition, even the brief kind that flickers across someone's face, can feel like being held, a confirmation of existence. I let myself accept it without judgement. Maybe ego and sincerity are not opposites after all, but two sides of the same human ache.

The school has no hierarchy, no rigid formality, only a gentle current of care. When I mentioned

Seven

that my bag had been stranded at the airport and the airline refused to bring it to me, they didn't hesitate. Within minutes, someone was already arranging to fetch it on my behalf, sparing me the long, chaotic drive through the valley. Their kindness is simple, unceremonious, the kind that expects nothing in return.

Before I arrived, Bhuwanji had told me they'd opened a restaurant at the front of the school. The thought had filled me with a strange nervousness. I wondered if the old walls had been torn down and what remained of the building I once knew. What would be of the room I had recognised as my own?

I was relieved to see the house remained unchanged. I longed to see my old room again. It is difficult to explain such an attachment, even here in Rishikesh. Bhuwanji offered to show me around. I asked if we might go first to the room behind the wooden doors. He didn't question my request. True to his nature, he simply nodded and led the way.

For a moment I stood still, letting memory settle over me like the embrace of an old friend. As I stepped into the small room at the heart of the house, the familiarity that had once wobbled my foundations no longer haunted me in the same way. Curiosity rose where fear used to live, and I felt an ease, a willingness to look directly at what might never be seen or answered by logic.

Surrender is not a permanent state, at least not until it is. But once you have tasted it, even briefly, you carry a quiet peace in your bones, a steady knowing that such freedom exists. Something in you remains cracked open to possibility. You no longer cling so tightly to the identity you spent years crafting. Or to the one the world insists on reflecting back at you.

Upstairs, a new yoga hall had taken root, a wooden and steel treehouse with a high ceiling and large windows looking out toward the Ganga. Like the school, I too had grown in our time apart. Now returning as a mother.

My body had been tugged, stretched, torn and stitched, reshaped by the ancient alchemy of bringing life into the world. The thread I had sewn here in Rishikesh seven years before, the one that held my mind and body in union, had split. My spiritual practice had thinned, then disappeared into the fog of feeding schedules and broken sleep. Even the bindi that used to sit at the centre of my forehead, my small north star, my inner compass, had slipped away. I hadn't even noticed when she left.

Even in that thinning, something remained. A quiet pulse beneath the noise of responsibility and routine. Now back where it had all begun, I could see it was not gone, only waiting.

It had been hiding in the shadows and as I stood there bathing in the light of the Himalayan sun, it came into view. As though I'd stepped into an old Disney animation, leaves swirling around me, animals gathering, some magical melody rising from nowhere. An instinct of knowing returned. I had seven days. Seven precious days to return, to reconnect, to remember myself.

Seven days to feel once again, the quiet serenity of being whole.

TANTRA

There will always be a place for those who choose the path of renunciation. For those called to monasteries and mountain caves, to silence and solitude. The classical path holds withdrawal as the route to transcendence. But it is not the only one. Some of us are not destined to transcend this physical world.

For a long time, I had seen my journey into yoga as a staircase, each course or retreat a step towards knowing. But I now see I hadn't been climbing at all. I'd been circling, spiralling around the same centre, each turn revealing a wider pattern beneath. It was tantra that held these threads together, the underlying rhythm connecting everything I had learnt.

My dharma has revealed itself through service and sleepless nights, in hospitals thick with the scent of humanity, during night feeds of devotion and in the rare stillness of a yoga retreat.

Tantra yoga meets me here, where I am. It doesn't ask me to rise above life but to step more deeply into it. It teaches me that everything, every challenge, every joy, every mundane repetition, is made of the same divine fabric. The world is not *Māyā* to be transcended but *Śakti* to be experienced, honoured, and understood.

Tantra invites participation, not withdrawal. It doesn't divide spirit and matter but asks us to see through the illusion of separation. To live tantrically is to live awake inside the storm, to let the waves rise and fall without fear. It is to realise that liberation is not elsewhere, waiting in some future of perfect silence, but right here.

As women, we have long been scripted as the householders, the keepers of life, the tenders of continuity. In a world that once reserved enlightenment for those who could leave, renouncing the world in pursuit of the divine, tantra offered a doorway for those who stayed. A path that didn't require abandonment, one that saw the sacred in nurturing and in returning again and again to the same daily rhythms with awareness.

During one of my visits to Rishikesh in the years prior, I had learned that the divine does not dwell only in temples or chants, but in the women who dance when the world tells them to be still.

The ashram was smaller this time, tucked into the hillside above Tapovan, where the mountains pressed close, shielding it from the noise of the world. Its walls were the colour of warm turmeric, the floors cool stone beneath bare feet.

I had come to learn the dance of Shiva (Śiva) and Shakti (Śakti), the eternal interplay of masculine and feminine, consciousness and creation. When I arrived, the philosophy quickly gave way to something far more alive.

At first, I was the only guest. The ashram was quiet; the teacher was bound to a vow of silence, breaking it only in brief murmurs during class. The stillness was not the serenity I had imagined; it felt hollow, almost accusing.

I had come seeking truth but instead found the uneasy echo of my own motives. I wondered if I had been chasing something less pure than I wanted to believe. Had I come for spiritual awakening, or for belonging, the gentle intoxication of community, affirmation, and purpose. Without the crowd, the chanting, the shared rhythm of others, what remained of my devotion. I sat on the edge of my bed, unsure whether to stay or go.

Like birds released from a cage, five women arrived in a burst of colour and laughter. All from Tehran, their English hesitant but their joy fluent. On that first evening one of them, Leila, whose English was more fluent than the others, whispered as we walked between class and the dinner hall, *"Our husbands think we are in Istanbul, shopping."* She laughed, her eyes glinting with rebellion.

I did not understand when they spoke among themselves, but I could feel the sense of mischief and defiance in their voices. In Iran, Leila told me, "We cannot dance. We cannot not sing. We cannot not let our hair blow in the wind."

The next evening on the terrace as the sun set, with the fragrance of humid soil in the air, I watched their headscarves slipping, their hands tracing invisible circles in the air, feet bare against the stone. A phone delivering a simple drumbeat. I felt the envy of someone who had always been free, but never truly wild.

That day we had been taught in class that tantra was about presence, about meeting life with such honesty, that even desire becomes a prayer. Shakti (Śakti), the divine feminine, is not submissive, but fierce and creative, the power that keeps the universe spinning. Our teacher said:

"When you suppress the body, you silence Śakti herself."

The Iranian women nodded. Their eyes shone with something ancient. I thought of all the rules that bind us, visible or not. My own moral code, ideals of modesty and colonial politeness. Wondering how many had been self-imposed.

The next morning, we sat in the garden, jasmine in the air; someone poured chai into small metal cups. Leila turned to me and said, *"Back home we are ghosts; here we are alive."* Her words lingered like a bruise beneath the skin.

At first, I felt shame burn quietly beneath my ribs, not for what I had done, but for what I had never had to do. For all I had taken for granted.

Then gratitude came as I let the judgement pass, my vision widening enough to recognise how much of my life had been softened by privilege. I have learnt how judgement and guilt pull the self, the I, the me back to the centre of the frame. What followed was different, not guilt, but awareness. Not self-reproach, but an acceptance that allowed me to see further.

Almost a decade later I was back in the ashrams of Rishikesh once again, walking into the last dance of my retreat. The air was heavy with the scent of rain, and the sun rays flooded the hall. A low pulse from the music vibrated up through the floor. My feet were rooted, each movement a surrender rather than a performance. Outside, a double rainbow arched over the valley, two perfect ribbons of colour. I thought about the women from Tehran. They danced not to seduce but to reclaim the right to feel alive inside their own skin.

Only now could I see that what I had been learning all along was tantra.

Tantra rarely wears its own name. It has been misread so many times that even here on my dance retreat the word was absent in the title. Teachers hesitate to use the word, afraid its meaning will be lost beneath misunderstanding.

In the West, the word has been reduced to a whisper of the erotic, its sacred geometry flattened into a marketing slogan. But the truth I glimpsed that night had nothing to do with indulgence. And everything to do with intimacy. Intimacy with life itself.

Centuries ago, colonial eyes once looked upon tantra as a savage ritual to be tamed. The mantras, the mingling of flesh and spirit, were held up as proof of the depravity of Hindus and the imagined darkness from which Christianity had come to deliver them. British missionaries wrote of tantra with horror, describing it not as a sacred path but as a moral failure.

It was the perfect contrast to the whiteness and purity of Christianity, the empire's chosen symbol of salvation. The bride's dress, the shade of restraint, of innocence preserved. Beneath its quiet moral code runs the belief that purity must be protected from the mess of desire, from the body's unpredictable hunger.

We are taught to fear the heat of our own aliveness, to tidy passion into silence and call it grace. Our moral architecture depends on a civilisation built, on the repression of its own pulse. Womanhood reinforces that compliance is the path to safety. We are conditioned to distrust our own vitality, in the taming of instinct and a quiet choreography of restraint.

We soften our anger and lower our voices. We've learned to shrink rather than take up space, to be neat, agreeable, careful not to be too much. Not too loud, not too wild, not too vulgar. Those unspoken rules settled into our bodies long before we recognised them as rules at all. They curled into our shoulders and stitched themselves into the restraint with which we try to inhabit the world.

There are moments I still replay: times I didn't speak, didn't challenge, didn't risk the discomfort. In meeting rooms where men interrupted women and I said nothing. In ambulance mess rooms where a crude joke was passed off as banter and I looked away. Each time I told myself it wasn't worth the confrontation, that silence was the higher ground. Looking back, my silence was not grace but fear. Fear of being called difficult, of being dismissed, of losing the fragile approval that polite women are trained to protect. Reluctance to disturb the peace isn't personal to me; it's endemic in my culture, in my whiteness.

Tantra unravels this inheritance; it whispers that liberation begins not in the overthrow of others but in the soft dismantling of our own obedience. The deepest chains are rarely external; they're the ones we've learned to tighten ourselves. In their loosening, we question the reflexes that once kept us safe but now keep us small. We desire to reclaim the parts of ourselves we exiled in order to be accepted.

Perhaps that is why the West became so captivated by tantra. It offered what our pale morality had denied, permission to be whole. Then the same gaze turned it into an exotic promise of deliverance. What was once feared as sinful became sold as sensual, a promise of sacred sex and candlelit liberation.

It was in truth never about indulgence but integration, remembering that the sacred does not live apart from the body, but within it. Whether through conquest or consumption, the West's fascination with tantra has always revealed less about the practice and more about itself.

In tantra, the divine feminine is not a metaphor but the very pulse of creation. The goddess is not symbolic of power; she is power.

Throughout history, the divine feminine has been worshipped and feared. The priestesses of the ancient temples, the healers of the old forests, all once keepers of sacred knowledge, were later branded witches. Whatever her name, she has been repeatedly sanctified, then vilified. Tantra understands the body as holy in its entirety. Blood, birth, decay, desire are all part of its sacred architecture. The West, unable to imagine holiness in flesh, turned the goddess into temptation. Devotion collapsed into objectification.

As the beat of the dance quickened, I realised the tension I had carried into Rishikesh seven days earlier had dissolved. The ache that had settled deep in my pelvis, the dull tug of scar tissue that no stretch or pose could soothe, was gone. My body, which had once felt like a vault of memory, had softened.

Two years before, I had laid on an operating table, the metallic echo of instruments cutting through the room, whilst the hospital intercom repeating the words *"maternity major trauma call."* I watched the trembling hands search for a vein in my arm. As a paramedic, I knew with cruel clarity what that meant. The protocols that followed and that my survival was balancing on a thin line, measured in seconds and blood pressure readings.

They told me later there were no lasting physical effects of blood loss, that as long as you survive, you can escape without injury. Until the moment I felt life draining out of me, slipping like sand through cupped hands, I too would have agreed. But surviving is not the same as returning. Some part of me had stayed hovering in that sterile air, caught between worlds, unsure how to come back into a body that had both held and betrayed me.

Women's pain has always been edited for palatability, translated into silence or self-blame. Medicine, for all its science, still carries the residue of a theology that sees female suffering as natural, even necessary. Across waiting rooms and wards, women are told their symptoms are exaggerated, their instincts unreliable, their thresholds too low.

We are praised for endurance, not listened to for warning. As though our capacity to bear pain is proof of resilience rather than evidence of neglect. The body that bleeds, births and feeds, labelled as demanding when it speaks too loudly of its own limits.

And I know this too. If I had been a woman of colour, my chances of surviving that night would have been lower. Black women in the UK are still four times more likely to die in childbirth than white women. It is not biology that determines this, but bias. The systemic disbelief of pain that is not white. *Are these the shadows of an empire still at work, where some bodies are deemed resilient enough to suffer?*

Excuse me, if I want to come back to my body, to bow to her with reverence, to listen when she aches, to follow when she calls. I have spent too many years silencing her, performing, mistaking numbness for strength. So yes, I will feel, I will desire, I will move deeper into the pulse of my own aliveness and call it tantra. I am done making myself small for the comfort of those who fear women who know their own power.

AUTHOR.

A friend once told me he wanted a tattoo that said, *"When life gives you lemons, make lemonade."* I remember thinking how much that saying is about perspective. I have always loved lemons, bright as sunlight, unapologetically vivid. So sharp they make your cheeks ache, the way an unrestrained laugh does. Lemonade, by contrast, never held the same magic for me. Murky, overly sweet, its spirit watered down, often sealed in plastic. But as with so many repeated wisdoms, the origins of the saying had been shaped over time:

"He picked up the lemons that fate had sent him and started a lemonade-stand."
Elbert Hubbard, The Fra, 1915

Lemons, it turns out, were not something bad, to be turned into something good, but an opportunity to start something new. Perhaps my friend had known this all along. We all interpret language differently, translating words into the private dialogue of our own minds. Idioms do not live on the page alone, their meaning is completed by the reader, shaped by memory, temperament, and maybe even their appetite.

Before I ever imagined this book into existence, two events occurred like signposts on my path. Without them, these words would never have found their way here. The first came disguised as disappointment. I found myself an applicant in a recruitment process, which was investigated for possible corruption, an experience that nudged me back to my part-time role on the ambulance. The second was far more ordinary in appearance, a flight change, a reshuffled itinerary, resulting in a nine-hour layover in Delhi.

Both were in fact gifts of time. Time often feels like it is slipping through my fingers, as I rush from one commitment to the next and watch my children age before me. Yet that day in Delhi, time arrived uninvited, and if I'm honest, a little unsettling.

Stillness has never come easily to me. With ADHD, empty hours can feel like a cliff-edge. Too much space for my mind to scatter, too much room for thoughts to sprint in every direction at once.

Writing a book had lived on my bucket list for as long as I could remember, but it had felt like a pipedream. An unfinished story, stacked on the shelf beside the many half-read books that accompanied me through life. But there suspended between flights I found the enough space to set this idea alight.

Once the seed of this book took root in my mind, I found myself locked in with a kind of focus we're often told we lack. This is one of the great misunderstandings of ADHD, that it is a deficit of attention. In truth, it's attention that refuses to stay where the dopamine is scarce. However, when fire of a passion is lit, the focus becomes fierce, unwavering, almost monastic in nature.

Sat on a brown leather seat with cold metal armrests in the departures terminal of Delhi airport, I scribbled feverishly in a small notebook gifted by the ashram. Moving only to shift my weight, relieving a numb limb now and then. People around me came and went, lives passing in fast-forward, while I remained paused in a pocket of time. I was locked inside a bubble of words; the world blurred at the edges. Until I looked up and met the gaze of a young girl, perhaps seven or eight years old.

Her mother was occupied with two younger children. She sat there patiently waiting, her eyes fixed on me. I smiled at her, and she offered a shy smile back. It wasn't the writing that fascinated her; it was me. I could see in the reflection of her eyes that it was my whiteness. The world had woven a tale for her in which girls like me were placed on a pedestal, bathed in borrowed light.

Her wonder wasn't personal; it was inherited, absorbed from a world that had long narrated who deserves your attention. In her eyes, I saw not a child's curiosity but the long shadow of a world that scripts us before we can speak. And in that brief exchange, the title *Not Another White Girl* was born.

We do not meet as blank pages. We are palimpsests. Our lives are written over with the pigment of history. And as I stepped back from the encounter with the young girl, I felt the tug of recognition that this was not a single moment but one thread in a vast tapestry I had rarely dared to examine. The stories projected onto me, and the scripts I had slipped into without resistance. They have been shaping the rooms I entered and the person I believed myself to be.

We are all labelled by the assumptions of others. Sometimes they pass us by unnoticed, and others jolt us into the room with a sharp sting. The day I walked into the office of a private GP to complete my medical for my C1 driving licence was one of those days.

The doctor looked up from his desk as I walked into the room, looked me straight in the eyes and said, "let me guess, horse box?" At first, I was puzzled by the remark, not armed with a response. I did what every polite woman is taught to do in these circumstances and gave back a half laugh, laced with an appeasing smile.

Of course, he felt safe to continue, "Well it's not going to be a HGV, is it?" laughing to himself, seemingly pleased with his assumed wit. As the little fire of defiance burnt through my polite conditioning, my posture changed and my eyes met his with force, no more comforting smiles available. "Ambulance," I replied.

Author.

Whilst working in the ambulance service, I have experienced many of these sharp moments of awakening. But not all have been so obvious, my most recent experience took its time to surface, harder to explain but no less real. These are the kind that make you question your sanity and haunt you as you try to sleep at night.

It was not until the ground shifted, from privilege to exclusion, that I felt the weight of the reality I'd often been spared. To be misunderstood, yet placed on a pedestal you never asked for, is irritating at best. But to be discriminated against, to lose out on what you have earned because of someone's bias, conscious or unconscious, chips away at the soul.

That said, the lived reality for many is that discrimination does not just deny you opportunities; it can also deny your dignity, safety, and, for some, even life itself. There is a kind of prejudice so deep-rooted that it doesn't just wound; it destroys. When bias becomes a death sentence, the injustice can no longer pass as a white lie; it is tragic, unforgivable, and stains us all.

A few years earlier, I walked into my local Tesco off Brixton Hill, and the familiar face behind the counter was upset and being consoled by a colleague. I overheard her say, *"Why do they always think black men are dangerous? I'm so scared for my boys."* Chris Kaba and I shopped at the same Tesco. She remembered his face. This was 2 years after the world had learnt the name George Floyd.

I wanted to believe that I was different. I didn't carry the biases that were being revealed to us day after day in the news. I wasn't the sort of white person who would judge a person as more dangerous based on the colour of their skin. After all, my childhood image of a black man was Akee, a vision of safety and protection.

However, I have learned that racism is not a storm that rages only in other people's skies. It is a mist that settles quietly over us all, so familiar we no longer notice its dampness on our skin. It seeps into language, into stories, into the way we learn to see and not see one another.

If I do not name my own privilege as part of this weather, if I pretend, I am somehow exempt, then I will never unlearn the conditioning that shaped me. And without unlearning, there can be no awakening, no clearing of the fog, no truer way of seeing.

Spiritual practice has been my tool into a conscious state of living, where loving thy neighbour doesn't feel like a commandment but a state of being. In a world increasingly intent on dividing us, the practice of yoga feels more vital than ever. It calls us to reconcile the parts of ourselves that we have exiled, to create peace within, so that we might extend it outwards.

When we are at ease with our own imperfections, we are able to see them not as personal failings but as reflections of our social conditioning. From that place, we can remain open to challenge, to transformation, to one another.

Our communities shape us, our values, our identities, and the stories we tell about ourselves. We can't escape social conditioning; none of us grows up in a vacuum, but we can choose to expand it. When we place ourselves among people who stretch our thinking rather than shrink it, our minds begin to open in ways we didn't know were possible.

There is a revolution in our midst, one that teaches self-love. The rebel leader is Lu Featherstone, a self-love coach and empowerment activist whose mission is to help women reclaim their power, confidence and bodies. Travelling the country in a vintage American school bus she lovingly calls Susie, adorned in bright leopard-print and bold colours. This is no longer just a vehicle; it's a pilgrimage on wheels.

Once a vicar's daughter, raised on hymns and Sunday sermons. She has become her own kind of minister in adulthood. Through her, women learn to remember themselves, not the obedient versions the world prefers, but their unruly, shimmering selves. The summer before writing this book, I spent four glorious days with her and 50 inspiring women in a field in Bedfordshire. The women shared their achievements, not as status, but as guides showing the way. I came away from that week believing with child-like openness I could do anything, maybe even write a book!

We are built for togetherness. From the moment we're born, our survival depends on the warmth of another's gaze. When you set yourself free, allow your light to burn bright, not only is anything possible, but it's also one hell of a ride.

Choose a life that is right for you.
Choose friends who fan your flames.
Choose Love always x

Printed in Dunstable, United Kingdom